PSYCHOLOGY RESEARCH PROGRESS

PLACEBO EFFECTS

CLINICAL ASPECTS, METHODOLOGICAL APPROACHES AND ETHICAL IMPLICATIONS

PSYCHOLOGY RESEARCH PROGRESS

Additional books in this series can be found on Nova's website under the Series tab.

Additional e-books in this series can be found on Nova's website under the e-book tab.

PSYCHOLOGY RESEARCH PROGRESS

PLACEBO EFFECTS

CLINICAL ASPECTS, METHODOLOGICAL APPROACHES AND ETHICAL IMPLICATIONS

KENDRA VAUGHN
EDITOR

New York

Library of Congress Cataloging-in-Publication Data

Placebo effects : clinical aspects, methodological approaches and ethical implications / Kendra Vaughn, editor.
pages cm. -- (Psychology research progress)
Includes index.
ISBN 978-1-63482-960-1 (softcover)
1. Placebos (Medicine) I. Vaughn, Kendra.
RM331.P54 2015
615.5--dc23

2015017725

Published by Nova Science Publishers, Inc. † New York

CONTENTS

Preface		**vii**
Chapter 1	Placebo Effect in Complementary and Alternative Medicine (CAM) and Homeopathy *Salvatore Chirumbolo*	**1**
Chapter 2	The Placebo and Nocebo Responses in Patients with Epilepsy *Fabio Giovannelli, Filippo Sean Giorgi and Gaetano Zaccara*	**47**
Chapter 3	Nocebo Phenomena: 'Negative Non-Specific Effects' *Maddy Greville-Harris and Paul Dieppe*	**61**
Index		**81**

PREFACE

Placebo effect is a medical term indicating an effect attributed to sham pharmaceutical preparations, which are able to induce a positive or a recovery response in an individual interacting both with placebo and the general practitioner, physician or caregiver. The placebo response is a well-recognized phenomenon, particularly in the context of clinical trails. The chapters in this book examine the recent debate about the role of placebo in pharmacology, particularly in neuro-pharmacology, psychology and palliative care in cancer and has shed a light on the placebo component of CAM (complementary and alternative medicine) and the use of placebo in evidence based medicine (EBM). The authors' of the second chapter look at the putative mechanisms of placebo and nocebo responses in epilepsy, which are hypothesized and discussed along with possible consequences in clinical practice. The third chapter provides a brief discussion of the ethical and clinical implications of the nocebo response.

Chapter 1 - Placebo effect is a medical term indicating an effect attributed to sham pharmaceutical preparations, which are able to induce a positive or a recovery response in an individual interacting both with placebo and the general practitioner, physician or caregiver. Therefore, according to a classical model of social psychology, such a relationship might contribute to either a placebo or nocebo effect, namely an improvement or a pejorative status in the individual undergoing therapy. Placebo response has come to the spotlight fundamentally in complementary and alternative medicine (CAM). Negative expectations deriving from the clinical interview might produce negative outcomes, known as nocebo effects, which, if occurring, could be misunderstood as therapy-related adverse effects or as a pathway obliged to occur because of the homeostatic response from the subject. This is particularly important in CAM approaches and in homeopathy. Specifically, research on the nocebo effect is poorly represented in alternative and complementary medicine (CAM), where people's expectations about healing and cure overwhelm any nocebo and side effect towards a placebo performance. Recent debate about the role of placebo in pharmacology, particularly in neuro-pharmacology, psychology and palliative care in cancer has shed a light on the placebo component of CAM and the use of placebo in evidence based medicine (EBM) and expanded the debate about their role in pharmacology and clinics. This chapter tries to elucidate these issues.

Chapter 2 - Placebo and nocebo responses in epilepsy have been mainly investigated by meta-analytic approaches aimed to evaluate the extent of such phenomenon in randomized, controlled, clinical trials. These studies reported placebo response rates (defined as proportion of patients with ≥ 50% improvement of seizures compared to baseline observations) ranging from 9.9% up to 15.2%. The proportion of patients with adverse events (AEs) and those withdrawing because of intolerable AEs, as index of nocebo response, were 60.3% and 3.9%, respectively. Moreover, a full evaluation of specific AEs reported by patients receiving placebo has been performed. A number of factors related to the features of patients (severity of disease), to the study design, or to non-specific factors (such as year of publication and geographic area), as well as to positive or negative expectations of patients, caregivers and experimenters have been showed to influence placebo and nocebo response in epilepsy. A characterization of these factors is crucial for a better interpretation of study results and to improve design of new clinical trials. All recent data will be presented and discussed in detail.

In addition, as neurobiological studies in epilepsy are lacking, putative mechanisms of placebo and nocebo responses in epilepsy will be hypothesized and discussed along with possible consequences in clinical practice.

Chapter 3 - The placebo response (improvement in disease or illness in response to an intervention with no active ingredient) is a well-recognised phenomenon, particularly in the context of clinical trials. Its opposite (worsening in response to an 'inactive' intervention) is less well documented and understood, in part because of the difficulties encountered in studying it. However, there is now a considerable literature reporting nocebo responses in trials, in response to medication prescriptions, as well as in response to population-based activities such as the introduction of mobile phones. In addition, and given emphasis in this article, a well-intentioned health care consultation can result in negative outcomes.

The authors' research has investigated the role of invalidation, and of feeling unsafe or threatened, on the induction of a nocebo response. The authors' work has led them to believe that it is easier to induce a negative response than a positive one within healthcare consultations, and that nocebo is more powerful than placebo ('bad is more powerful than good').

The authors conclude with a brief discussion of the ethical and clinical implications of the nocebo response.

In: Placebo Effects
Editor: Kendra Vaughn
ISBN: 978-1-63482-960-1

Chapter 1

PLACEBO EFFECT IN COMPLEMENTARY AND ALTERNATIVE MEDICINE (CAM) AND HOMEOPATHY

Salvatore Chirumbolo, Ph. D.
Department of Medicine, University of Verona, Italy

ABSTRACT

Placebo effect is a medical term indicating an effect attributed to sham pharmaceutical preparations, which are able to induce a positive or a recovery response in an individual interacting both with placebo and the general practitioner, physician or caregiver. Therefore, according to a classical model of social psychology, such a relationship might contribute to either a placebo or nocebo effect, namely an improvement or a pejorative status in the individual undergoing therapy. Placebo response has come to the spotlight fundamentally in complementary and alternative medicine (CAM). Negative expectations deriving from the clinical interview might produce negative outcomes, known as nocebo effects, which, if occurring, could be misunderstood as therapy-related adverse effects or as a pathway obliged to occur because of the homeostatic response from the subject. This is particularly important in CAM approaches and in homeopathy. Specifically, research on the nocebo effect is poorly represented in alternative and complementary medicine (CAM), where people's expectations about healing and cure overwhelm any nocebo and side effect towards a placebo performance. Recent debate about the role of placebo in pharmacology, particularly in neuro-pharmacology, psychology and palliative care in cancer has shed a light on the placebo component of CAM and the use of placebo in evidence based medicine (EBM) and expanded the debate about their role in pharmacology and clinics. This chapter tries to elucidate these issues.

INTRODUCTION

The term *placebo* means literally "I shall please" and refers to a sham pharmacological treatment that is intended to provoke a positive outcome in a consulting patient. In this perspective, a placebo always needs a patient/practitioner relationship (PPR), as placebo does not contain any therapeutic information aside from this relationship. Whether or not the placebo may generate a biological effect due to its chemical or biochemical intrinsic property, fundamentally the medical explanation of its presumptive efficacy cannot do without the full consideration of PPR in the observed therapeutic potential. Interestingly, the term "I shall" within the original meaning of placebo, suggests for an expectation from the patient, which could be translated even as "I shall heal", "I shall feel better". In this approach, even the simple PPR without any "material thing" warranting for patient trusting this relationship, might generate a placebo effect. This would mean that any drug, intended to work according to a defined biochemical mechanism and bearing a defined chemical activity, might generate a placebo effect that should even improve its therapeutic action, if prescribed through an optimal PPR mechanism. The concept of placebo in pharmacology is currently affected by a reductionisti prejudice, as placebo is simply used to indicate any harmless or chemically inert compound able to induce a positive response in the treated patient. This consideration has been included in any scientific explanation of presumptive positive evidence reported in complementary and alternative medicine (CAM), especially homeopathy. A placebo effect, even during PPR in a CAM mediated therapy, should arise from the relationship coming from the practitioner towards the patient (counselling stage or consultancy) and from the staunch awareness of patients on the healing potential of the CAM therapy prescribed by that practitioner (trust stage). Placebo needs fundamentally the counselling stage (consultancy), as the personal, single and autonomous conviction about the efficacy of a remedy might not elicit a placebo response, without an authorative, expert, legal and unbiased recommendation, and yet even reading drug instruction carefully prior to use, especially if warnings are particularly reassuring for health recovery and are technically endowed, may generate a placebo response, which is immediately effective as much as the individual experienced a positive outcome with that therapy. Placebo is a mechanism that is caused by a complex pattern of neuro-physiological active molecules, mainly neuropeptides, is inter-related with immune homeostasis and metabolic/energetic balance and therefore is a complex product of the so-called "relationship life". Its onset occurs quite specifically in the context of a dialogic relationship; therefore the perception of social interactions plays a major role in the generation of a placebo response. Yet placebo is a term most frequently adopted in CAM and homeopathy and in this sense a clarification is undoubtedly necessary.

2. Placebo in CAMs, Homeopathy and Palliative Care

2.1. Background

Placebo is a major object of discussion in any debate involving comments and evidence dealing with complementary and alternative medicine (CAM), particularly for homeopathy [1-4]. The consideration that, at least theoretically, the homeopathic therapy called *remedy* does not contain any sizable active principle, prompts researcher to believe that a therapeutic effect, if any, may come quite exclusively from a placebo effect in a PPR-mediated mechanism, particularly in pathologies with an evident psychosomatic or mental cause [5-8]. The homeopathic remedy is comparable to an inert chemical component, although no molecule has to be considered ineffective at all when interacting with a complex living organism, but, fundamentally, homeopathy funds its basic chemistry on liquid water or sugar globules, both essentially harmless, highly well tolerated and pharmacologically inactive chemical species. The attempt of homeopathy to demonstrate a therapeutic mechanism aside from placebo, characterizes most of reports currently expanding the debate about the pharmacological and medical plausibility of this practice [9-14]. Notwithstanding, many homeopaths trust PPR as the main therapeutic vehicle, despite the physical remedy and often attaining to odd theories and speculations [15, 16]. Yet, homeopaths and researchers investigating homeopathy are not inclined to use the concept of placebo in their practice and study [17] Fundamentally, they do not believe that remedies may work almost exclusively as placebos, as a placebo effect is mainly claimed by researchers who clearly express their scepticism towards CAM and homeopathy [18, 19]. However, placebo was introduced in homeopathy just at the beginning of its foundation by C.H.S. Hahnemann (1755-1843) [20] and in this sense physicians meeting this new adopted medical practice and tenet should take into account both placebo, as a sham therapy, and the placebo effect, caused by sham therapy within a PPR mechanism. The pharmacological background of a placebo as a therapy becomes quite puzzling when chemical systems, theoretically containing few or no molecule within, are used as therapeutic drugs: the simple fact that the therapy does not contain any active principle prompts physicians to attribute to that compound a placebo effect, despite any consideration about the PPR context. Obviously this should be considered an over-simplification.

2.2. Placebo and Homeopathy at the Beginning: The "Innocent Deception": Sham Placebo or Type 1 Placebo (PL1)

A possible date of birth for homeopathy is next to the end of Napoleonic era, when a conference of ambassadors of European states, chaired by the Austrian statesman KW von Metternich and held in Vienna from September 1814 to June 1815, changed the political landscape of Europe for at least one century. Actually, C.H.S. Hahnemann, the forerunner and founder of this medical practice, began its systematic approach made by serial dilutions and strong mechanical stress on the liquid solvent ("succussions") in 1814 [21, 22]. Placebo was introduced in medical therapy and in a first attempt of randomized clinical trials by the first half of the XIX century [22-24] but its involvement in medicine actually goes back to the end of the XVIII century [20, 25, 26]. Most probably, the term placebo was used for the first time in 1772 by W. Cullen (1710-1790) [23]. At that time, pharmacology in medicine took the first steps [27, 28] but while endeavouring to promote new efficacious drugs with known chemicals, toxicological problems were yet far to be successfully addressed. At the end of XVIII century, placebo was introduced to face at this main concern and it does not matter if prescription of placebo might be potentially noxious or simply ineffective, the main thing considered by doctors was that the patient went on with trusting the physician and his prescription, in order to warrant healing and wellbeing. Diluting chemical materials, in order to highly reducing the toxic action of a "remedy", certainly was the simplest approach used to prevent possible iatrogenic damages.

Therefore, two distinct natures of placebo arose in that time: placebo from sham medicine (chemically inert compounds) and placebo from high diluted chemically active compounds. In the first case, placebo was used as it occurs in palliative care and can be classified as a type 1 placebo or PL1. Although this kind of placebo was introduced to dismiss boring and hypochondriacal subjects from stressing medical consultation, placebo from a whatsoever diluted active principle appears to be a main quality of homeopathy [26]. While most of general practitioners at the end of the XVIII century came across with the "deceptive" concept of placebo, Hahnemann used sham medicine as placebo, mostly represented by milk sugar, apparently in order to prevent any side effect to patients. In his writings, Hahnemann himself tried to explain the reason why he replaced medicine with harmless nourishment (milk sugar, i.e. lactose), used as placebo, and actually milk sugar was frequently adopted by Hahnemann to dismiss anxious and boring patients. Jütte reported textually...*in the meantime, until the second medicament is given, one can soothe the patient's mind and desire for medicine with something inconspicuous such as a few teaspoons a day of raspberry juice or sugar of milk* [20, 29, 30] and moreover: *Patients who have firm confidence in the honesty and skill of their physician, will have no hesitation to be satisfied with a dose of sugar of milk, which may be exhibited every two, four, or seven days, agreeably to the wishes of the patient; such a course will never lessen their confidence...* [20]. This perspective may suggest that placebo effect proved as a fundamental concern in medical practice during the XIX century and probably the major target of medical therapy for chronic, highly complex pathologies involving psychic and mental stress, at least during those pioneering times [31]. Physicians and general practitioners used placebo as a legitimate fake, namely an "innocent deception on our hypochondriacal and fanciful patients" [32]. Although this statement may generate criticism about the ethical ground on which placebo was primarily intended, yet in the XIX century medicine lacked most of the current weapons against epidemics, toxicology, acute illness and particularly infectious diseases and main strategies pointed at checking and separating sick people from the community [33]. Furthermore, potentially noxious substances used as therapeutics, for example metals, salts or toxic alkaloids, whose healing potential was often presumptive and came quite exclusively from trusting the personal expertise of colleagues rather than experimental evidence, were diluted to prevent damage and ensure patients fundamentally a placebo effect, rather than a noxious action [34]. It is conceivable that homeopathy might have arisen in this context. The concept of mass dilution, rather than the "similia principle", probably prevailed in the common sense about homeopathy and therefore led to a fundamental misunderstanding yet present to date. Therefore, the "innocent deception" used to assuage stressed patients, may have some role in the intuitive tenet originating homeopathy in the XIX century; however, the nature of placebo in this approach is quite different respect to sham medicine. To date, PL1 is never used in homeopathy, as it is not included in any CAM therapy, beside palliative care. PL1 remains very interesting to highlight the neuro-physiological mechanism of sham medicine, as the ensuing placebo response should be almost completely attributed to PPR.

2.3. Placebo in the Chemical and Pharmacology Realm: Physical Placebo or Type 2 Placebo (PL2)

Interestingly, quantitative chemistry, stoichiometry and the Avogadro's principle arose and developed in the same amazing historical period, namely by the first half of the XIX century. When homeopathy was born, Hahnemann might have met Dalton's laws and Avogadro's principle, being all together contemporaries. Despite this, it may be highly implausible that Hahnemann completely understood and was fully aware of Avogadro's implications in quantitative chemistry and stoichiometry, as Avogadro's constant was defined by Perrin at the beginning of the XX century [35] and Avogadro's rules were misunderstood and their implications ignored until 1959 when it was introduced in the regular school education, yet the Avogadro's number and the concept of mole is difficult to comprehend even for modern students [36-38] and probably should undergo a reappraisal in the debate on homeopathy [39]. In this perspective, it is arguable that Hahnemann surely believed to the possibility that a highly diluted and strongly "energized" chemical preparation still bore a "pharmaceutical property". Therefore, it is also presumable that Hahnemann neither cared about a presumptive placebo effect in any of his remedy, at least as emerging from our modern concept of placebo as the only "active thing" presumably working from a highly diluted chemical activity, leading to the inert functional state. Although the most diffused opinion about homeopathy takes into consideration a possible placebo effect, this concept might be completely irrelevant to Hahnemann's conceiving about homeopathy and its basic tenet. Therefore, despite the fact that Hahnemann cannot be charged with having introduced a deceiving placebo effect in homeopathy, current medicine still has to address this concern. The introduction of a non sham placebo effect in pharmacology actually pertains to the sole homeopathy.

Tracing possible placebo-inducing mechanisms in homeopathy, more than in other CAM, obliges researchers to deepen the chemical physical issue of high diluted substances usually employed in homeopathic medicine. Noteworthy, Hahnemann never included the impact of a correct PPR mechanism in prescribing the remedy and making the effect of the latter a promising approach [29]. As many contemporary physicians, Hahnemann too carefully showed concern for those patients expressing ailments with particular emphasis: "*Besides this, patients themselves differ so much in their dispositions, that some, especially the so-called hypochondriacs and other persons of great sensitiveness and impatient of suffering, portray their symptoms in too vivid colors and, in order to induce the physician to give them relief, describe their ailments in exaggerated expressions*" (Hahnemann's Organon aphorisme 88 §96). This consideration suggests that in the XIX century placebo was never included in any therapeutic scheduling but yet as an innocent deception to reduce practitioner charge of patient claims.

When homeopathy conceived its *similia similibus curantur* tenet, by diluting substances supposed to be harmful in ponderal doses, medical observation of symptoms and their disappearance might have unconsciously included the effect of a placebo-inducing mechanism in their evaluation of health recovery or healing. We are currently unable to verify whether practitioners using homeopathy realized the possibility of a placebo effect during their successful practice. The best documented evidence about positive outcome in homeopathy comes from research investigating ailments with a high degree of spontaneous resolution or with a significant psychosomatic component [8, 40-42]. The awareness that a serial diluting process of a bioactive material leads to a chemical system characterized by a theoretical absence of any bio-active principle, has convinced people that if any positive outcome occurred, its explanation cannot be outside the involvement of a placebo mechanism. In this circumstance, medicine is all but a deception but its faded pharmacological activity makes them likewise a sham therapy. This new concept of placebo should take into account a stronger trust in a PPR mechanism, because the practitioner is believing the positive therapeutic action while prescribing the homeopathic medicine, contrarily to the sham medicine, where the physician knows very well it is a chemically inefficacious substance. Obviously, the first approach would enforce patient's trust on practitioner's counselling, resulting in the reception of many non verbal positive (encouraging) signals in a PPR-induced patient. Furthermore, most of homeopathic remedies come from natural sources. The idea of natural landscapes and natural sources should promote a complex of biopsychological signals activating a positive attitude towards patient's own ailment and the related prescribed therapy [43, 44]. This factor has to be added to the bio-psychic effect generated in a PPR mechanism by the cautelative, reassuring admission forwarded by the practitioner about the complete absence of adverse effects related to the prescribed therapy. The "placebo-inducing matter" or placebo inducing object (PIO) is made by a complex of signifying objects including:

(a) the existence of a thing bearing a therapeutic expectation (e,g. lactose globules)
(b) the awareness that this thing is a natural product;
(c) the trust that this thing is devoid of any adverse effect
(d) the direct or indirect experienced success of the prescribed therapy (the "thing").

In homeopathy, the placebo inducing mechanism should involve a vectorial dynamics including the existence of an object (thing), a positive awareness about its nature, the onset of a trusting attitude and the experience of a positive outcome. This vector is made by a PCDME-related process (**p**hysical, **c**onsciousness, **d**ecision **m**aking, **e**xperience of positive effect) and cannot generate any real placebo response without any of this component "acting consequently" within and along the vector; any placebo-like effect is therefore anticipatory of a true placebo mechanism, where wellbeing is the consequence of an immune homeostasis or immune successful response. As it will be further clarified below, consolidation of all these elements in the vector dynamics according to their sequence might lead to a bio-phychological mechanism, which we could identify as a placebo response to the therapy. However, taken together none of these PIOs may generate a placebo effect *per se* in the complete absence of a PPR mechanism or a trust source. A more general PPR mechanism, which we can define as HEIAR (**h**uman **e**nvironment/**i**ndividual **a**wareness **r**elationship), is a vectorial dynamics which generates trust on the remedy from the positive attitude towards known trustworthy people, as it occurs in social empathic interactions, not necessarily experts in the field but *experienced people of the positive outcome*. In this mechanism, components b) and c) might be more pronounced than a), which is almost completely replaced by d), as this relationship lacks the proper expertise about medicine and, in this sense, may generate doubts of its efficacy in the absence or weakness of d). This vector should lack any therapeutic expectation where b) and c) components warranted for trusting the therapeutic benefit, as it may be replaced by the strong conviction about the sure effectiveness of the therapy, as reported by trustworthy and convincing individuals. If the placebo mechanism is closely related to a PPR context, positive outcomes enhance the positive expectation on the defined remedy and increase the amount and frequency of positive attitudes towards the treatment, with the ensuing generation of a placebo response. Positive outcomes, whether attributed to a placebo effect, should be increased in a PL2 respect to a PL1, because of the highest frequency in bio-acting chemicals with possible effectiveness present in the treatment and the practitioner's strongest trust in treatment efficacy. As a matter of fact, PL2 is the most frequently placebo mechanism that can be claimed when CAM and homeopathy are used in the medical approach.

2.4. Placebo in Randomized Clinical Trials (RCTs) of Homeopathy: PL1, PL2 or Other? The Blinding Issue

Very few outstanding and scientifically sound papers in literature investigating homeopathy included randomized controlled trials versus placebo, most of which are meta-analyses [45-50]. Trials might be reported as a significant positive evidence yet despite the co-existence of confounders, such as the same placebo effect [51]. In clinical RCTs all placebos should be classified as PL1-like, i.e. fundamentally made by the inert vehicle devoid of the presumptive active principle. Blinding should prevent bias in the PPR mechanism if the practitioner *does not know anything* about the nature of what he is prescribing, except for its inert material, which represents a common substance shared with the therapy and taking part in a PIO. Blinding is a way to better randomize samples and the associated result (outcomes), in order to reduce bias and prevent confounders but particularly reduce PPR-related bias, where it is rather useless in *in vitro* studies [52]. Therefore, the best way to achieve this circumstance in clinical trials is to perform a randomized double blinded (RDB) approach. In this perspective, the term placebo is erroneously conceived, as a good RDB approach should wash out any effect due to a PPR mechanism, which might lead to a placebo response. Although placebo in RCTs may be considered a sham placebo, it is not a *real* PL1, because theoretically lacking of the classical PPR component.

When focusing on the nature of this new placebo, which will be classified as PL0, the participation of the PPR mechanism cannot be totally excluded, although significantly reduced. The practitioner is limited to make the patient simply believing the fact that the medicine *is a medicine,* surely with its curative expectation. Within the PPR mechanism at least three fundamental levels, besides the object or PIO, sequentially operate to generate trust in the patient: 1) welcome (anxiolytic); 2) awareness (empathy); 3) expectation (trust). These three levels parallel the vectorial steps b), c) and d) in a PCDME-related process. In a PL0 used for clinical RCTs component point 3) usually fails to warrant a trust mechanism, hence a possible placebo response. This should oblige researcher to revise the terminology of placebos in RCTs.

The sham inert vehicle might be considered a potent, efficacious medicine for the practitioner and consequently for the patient but a good randomized study depends on how much blinded are both people about the real nature of the drug and how the patient/practitioner communication develops in the course of trial. Therefore in this context, the PPR mechanism, though failing in its "trust" goal, is the only real confounder of the investigation, if we exclude other important biases coming from the historical background of the patient undergoing the study, randomization process, sampling, treatments and result management. The PPR environment, where any psychic response is elicited and moved on, is represented by whatsoever is considered a way of communicating and prescribing the drug (or placebo) to the patient, e.g. questionnaires and their questions/answers panel [53, 54].

In CAM and homeopathy the concept of placebo vs the homeopathic remedy is particularly puzzling because the PL2 component of a homeopathic medicine depends on the chemical size of the remedy. Interestingly, only "low potency medicines" [55] reported positive outcomes respect to "high potency" ones [56-59], while some paper did not specify the homeopathic dose [60]. Noteworthy, some RCTs has reported a positive outcome due to medical consultation rather than the prescribed therapy [61, 62]. The discouraging results coming from double blinded clinical RCTs of high diluted substances, having theoretical concentration of the presumptive active principle below nano- or picomoles/L, should suggest that the PPR-induced placebo effect in homeopathy is always possible [61] but should occurs exclusively in a neuro-psychic context, giving good expected results with psychosomatic pathologies such as irritable bowel syndrome or complex psycho-neuro-endocrine pathologies involving a chronic immune response. In this perspective, should CAM and particularly homeopathy be considered a "helpful" placebo or, rather, should prescribing an inert material to treat patients involve an unethical issue? [63, 64]. Yet to date, on the basis of the scanty bulk of clinical reports assessing the presumptive clinical efficacy of homeopathy, noone could wager exclusively on placebo to explain any positive outcome, as positive results might even depend on a) chemical activity of complex natural molecules (≥ 10 nmoles/L) in low potency homeopathic remedies; b) spontaneously occurring resolution; c) bias in the use of other functional complex molecules (vitamins, herbal supplements, drugs, etc..) before or during enrolment in the homeopathic treatment; d) bias in pooled statistics; e) direct anxiolytic, sedative effect of PPR (particularly in mood and somatoform disorders). This complex context can be explained with the fact that the psychological component of PPR on a patient undergoing blinded therapy with an inert material might have the same extend of placebo-inducer on a patient undergoing blinded therapy with a homeopathic high diluted remedy. Therefore, the arousal of typical psychic attitudes and emotions in patients undergoing the RCT vs placebo, may indifferently gather positive results either on a placebo-treated or homeopathy-treated group or both, depending on the impact of PPR and subject stratification (sex, age, cultural beliefs, and so forth). This renders RCTs in homeopathy particularly weak in the placebo vs non placebo statistics. The best protocol should prevent stratification bias, any evident confounder, correct sampling size (≥ 200 individuals) and drugs should be taken up by personal random choosing from an open-wide collection, without any PPR conditionally mechanism. For example, subjects recruited in the RCT, should be called, invited to complete a questionnaire (after the legitimate informed consent) and to choose a vial within a gross collection of identical vials, encompassing both placebo and therapy in a blinded random order. The idea of a placebo in CAM RCTs arises from orthodox pharmacology and EBM but homeopathic remedies do not behave as pharmacological systems, at least in the sub-nanomolar range. Therefore, many RCTs in homeopathy should be considered as blinded [PL2 vs PL1] clinical trials. Which is the "functional, working" therapeutic content of a PL2 respect to a PL1? This is particularly difficult to define. If we target the homeopathic remedy as a PL0 lacking chemical system and PL0 as a placebo, we might assume that PL0 *should certainly induce a placebo response* respect to the remedy. A good (testing sample vs control) rationale should highlight that "thing" possessed by the testing sample able to distinguish it from the control. In few words, in homeopathic double blinded RCTs, both remedy and PL0 might bear a *placebo inducing property* (PIP). Degree of PIP in any vial selected by the recruited subject within the trial closely depends on the PPR-related mechanism able to induce a placebo response and, as blinded PPR exerts its effect in a randomized fashion, statistical evaluation may reach easily a non significant value, leading to a negative outcome of the RCT. Conversely, the chemical activity of homeopathic remedy containing ponderal doses of herbal components, might make the difference. The degree of PIP could be very high for the inert material prescribed in a placebo inducing medical consultancy characterizing PPR. At least in theory, a cohort of patients could be treated with a placebo PL0 in a double blinded RCT and results elaborated at the end of the study. Positive outcomes should be all attributed to a placebo effect, due to medical consultancy. Obviously, this study design obliges researchers to be perfectly sure about the absolute absence of confounders, i.e. patients must neither be treated with nor assuming other substances aside from those ones indicated in the study, the effect of PPR should be evaluated according to stratified statistics if a good randomization has not been performed. Usually, if in this study design, a homeopathic remedy accounting for a chemical size below 1.0 pmol/L of its presumptive active principle is introduced in the RCT *in place of a* PL0, a researcher may achieve resulting evidence statistically comparable to that one obtained with only PL0. The extreme complexity of double blinded RCTs in CAM and homeopathy depends on the very little, hindering presumptive difference between two different testing substances having comparable degree of PIP, a difference that might be either enhanced by bias and confounders or dampened by a proper randomization process and subjects' complex response to the treatment. This occurrence, may explain why better RCTs in homeopathy were obtained with remedy *still* theoretically containing a bioactive molecule.

3. Placebo: Insights on the Neurophysiological Causes

3.1. Background

It is very difficult to elucidate the neuro-physiological mechanisms leading to a placebo response during medical consultancy in a PPR context or a HEIAR circumstance (see above). Suggestions may arise by taking into account endogenous neuropeptides able to relate neurophysiology with the immune function and also neuro-anatomical areas involved in modulating psychic response to stress, pain, fear and other emotional or rational arousals expected to occur within a dialogic dynamics with people proposing a therapy. In this neuro-psychic environment, what is defined as a *patient*, might undergo at least three separated steps towards a possible placebo response. These steps might involve an anxiolytic, sedation/coping mechanism, then an awareness stage and a trust-convinction level (memory-reward), where a good, efficacious placebo response should occur, with higher frequency, only when any of this level is accomplished in their vectorial sequence. Notwithstanding, in any of this level, particularly at the beginning, the patient can achieve an introductory mechanism leading to a "possible" placebo response but every step is anticipatory of the following. Therefore, while a sedate, non anxious individual might be prompted to be aware of the promising efficacy of the suggested therapy, neuro-physiological mechanisms might have prepared the subject to perform a better immune response and feel immediately better, because of the neuro-immune mechanisms modulating pain and anxiety. In few words, placebo should be identified as the mechanism leading to an immune resolution of the ailment through a neuro-physiological axis, while wellbeing, often mislead with a placebo effect, may derive exclusively from a psychological empathic arousal in a PPR context. This is a level that could warrant for the achievement of a placebo response if the PCDME process is properly led to its completion. Many neuro-active molecules may be involved in this complex mechanism but further insights are requested to better elucidate the issue.

3.2. PPR as an Anxiolytic Stimulus: The Placebo Introductory Mechanism

The mechanism eliciting a placebo response might involve an early anxiolytic and sedative action related to PPR dynamics. This anxiolytic stage may generate a placebo introductory mechanism, i.e. a neuro-immune event able to promote the introduction of an immune-mediated response, then resulting in the ensuing recovery of health or wellbeing. A simplistic, preliminary observation of how a placebo response may be aroused should take into consideration the ability of a consulting process to elicit the down-regulation of a stress and anxiogenic situation, allowing a neuro-endocrine mechanism able to modulate the immune function. Many factors, suggested below, might be involved in this complex function. Certainly, this should be considered as a "first step" in the possible placebo effect, leading to an immune resolution of the ailment, a condition called "introductory mechanism" to the placebo response. In this context, one may believe that PPR has a major role in the placebo-mediated healing process.

Particular pathologies and somatoform disorders might be addressed with a good prediction of positive outcome by psychological consultation as like as medical treatment. In this circumstance, as occurred with irritable bowel syndrome (IBS), recovery of a healthy condition might be erroneously attributed to homeopathy, if consultation in PPR is excellent [65]. Interestingly, the simple self-administered treatment did not ameliorate Quality Of Life (QoL) or distress, though improving gastro-intestinal symptoms, suggesting that consultation must play a major role in the anxiolytic effect of PPR [66]. Emotions are fundamental elements taking part in PPR dynamics and in the ensuing placebo mechanism. The human being shares with animals a primitive neural system for processing emotions such as fear and anger [67]. Fear is an instinct that can result in an anxiogenic mood disorder and it can put on the ground of every stressing situation where the subject is completely or almost completely unaware of the possible "end of his stress". Unlike other animals, humans possess the ability to control and modulate instinctive emotional reactions through intellectual processes such as reasoning, rationalizing or labelling their own experiences, all processes that are addressed in a PPR-mediated consultancy. By using functional MRI, Hariri and colleagues identified the neural networks characterizing this ability, involving left and right amygdale [67]. The neurobiology of the complex relationship between emotion and cognition may be a fundamental issue to comprehend how a placebo response arises in a PPR mechanism [68]. Furthermore, past reports have outlined a relationship between anxiety, mood disorders and immune system [69, 70] and therefore the possible anxiolytic property of a medical consultation in a PPR context might produce an immune response on the neuro-endocrine-immune axis [71-74]. Anxiety is a mood disorder that can be affected even by dis-regulated gut microbiota [75], therefore many complex factors might participate in a nocebo/placebo response in a PPR dimension.

Life stress and depression reduce the ability of immune response [76]. Anxiety has been strictly related to immune cells and brain. Brain mast cells participate in the modulation of anxiety-like disorders [77]. Neuro-endocrine stress response plays a major role in the biology of the immune system and the emotional state affects fundamentally leukocyte activity, trafficking and homing [78-80]. During a medical consultation, anxiety and stress related behaviours, may characterize patient's attitude towards the practitioner in the PPR context. It is very hard to foresee which kind of positive mechanism might be induced by the "empathic" relationship within the consulting environment but possible neuro-physiological issues can be addressed. Depending on the complex inter-relationship between brain and immunity, many neuropeptides and hormones might be suggested to be a possible cause or mediator of a placebo introductory response. The placebo introductory response involves mechanisms by which the individual undergoing consultation is setting the immune network to a pro-defensive response, either pro-inflammatory or immune down-regulatory. Endogenous glucocorticoids might play a major role in this context [81]. In stressed mouse models, although light cycle restraint were associated with changes in plasma corticosterone levels, the anxiolytic effect of dark cycle restraint occurred independently from plasmatic corticosterone [82], an evidence that would suggest that circulating corticosterone may be not directly related to an anxiolytic mechanism. Anyway, anxiolysis appear to be related to several neuropeptides, able to elicit an arousal in the immune response and downstream factors possibly involved includes also glucocoticoids, cortisol, adrenocorticotropic hormone (ACTH).. Many of these neuropeptides and hormones are actually associated to several complex neuro-physiological functions dealing with mood disorders and behaviour. For example, neuropeptide S (NPS) is the putative endogenous ligand of a G-coupled receptor (NPSR1) whose function is associated with anxiety reduction and corticosterone release [83]. This molecule has been recently associated to anxiety [84] and particularly the NPS/NPSR1 signaling has been related to the NSPR1 SNP-associated gastro-instestinal disorders [85]. Neuropeptide S has been actually reported as an anxiolytic promoting neuropeptide [86-88]. It is well known that many neuropepides are able to change gut lymphocyte phenotype and modulate gut immune function [89]. NPS is a regulator of pain-related amygdale activity on behaviour [90]; furthermore, the anxiolytic activity of the NPS/NPSR1 pathway seems to be mediated by ventral hippocampus [91, 92] and, as a neuropetide, it might participate in the control of regional immunity [93]. Animal models suggested a role of NPS in the immune system [94], therefore it is arguable that NPS might act at the crossroad between anxiety-mood behaviours and immunity and become a possible target neutopeptide for a placebo introductory response, as occurs with neuropeptide Y [95].

Neuropeptide Y (NPY-1-36), a pleiotropic neurohormone, has been associated to many functions related to metabolic/energetic and immune homeostasis, from control of obesity and cardiovascular function to anxiolysis [96]. This neuropeptide is considered the most abudant hormone-like peptide in central and peripheral nervous system. Its role in the immune function has been highlighted quite recently [97-98] and, despite its pleiotropism, it appears to directly modulate innate and acquired immunity, immune cell trafficking, T helper cell differentiation, cytokine secretion, natural killer cell activity, phagocytosis and the production of reactive oxygen species [99]. Its role in physiology emerged as a stress mediator of the neuro-psychic-endocrine-immune (NPEI) system but recently it was addressed as an important mediator of inflammation, whose action is implicated in autoimmune disorders, chronic allergy, metabolic and cardiovascular disease and even cancer [100-102]. Recently reported papers have shown that NPY induced a dose-dependent migration of human monocyte-derived immature DCs through the engagement of the NPY Y1 receptor and also the activation of ERK and p38 mitogen-activated protein kinases [100]. In addition, this neuropeptide promoted DC adhesion to endothelial cells and trans-endothelial migration but failed to induce phenotypic DC maturation, whereas it conferred a T helper 2 (Th2) polarizing profile to DCs through the up-regulation of interleukin IL-6 and IL-10 production [100]. NPY might regulate the neuro-physiological interaction between the anxiolytic process related to PPR and an immune response, then generating a placebo mechanism [103]. NPY is one of the major anxiolytic mediator able to cross act with immunity [104-105]. Its inhibitory activity on ACTH and cortisol, through an inhibition of the corticotropic releasing hormone (CRH) has been reported [106] and would suggest that NPY may activate immune responses, as ACTH usually depresses immunity [107]. Experimental studies with NPY and NPY receptor antagonists support the hypothesis that neuro-anatomy areas such the amygdale, the dorsal periaqueductal gray matter, locus coeruleus, the dorsocaudal lateral septum, represent a neuroanatomical substrate that should mediate the anxiolytic effect of NPY [108]. Although yet speculative, this evidence may support a possible relationship between anxiolytic effect and immune activation, through neuropeptides action.

Endogenous nociceptin/orphanin FQ is a 17-aa neuropeptide recently associated with the neuroendocrine stress response and exerting a wide range of neuro-modulatory functions, such as inflammation, immune homeostasis, anxiety and cognitive behaviour [109, 110]. The nociceptin receptor, known as ORL1, is ubiquitously present in the brain, namely many important CNS nuclei, spinal chord, hypothalamus, hippocampus and amygdale [111]. The role of this neuropeptidergic system has been recently associated to immunity, namely the activation of the N/OFQ-NOP pathway can regulate inflammatory and immune responses [112]. At least in laboratory animals, the nociceptin/orphanin FQ induces anxiolysis but this action should regard also humans [113-115], then this neuropeptide might be involved in a possible placebo effect during the anxiolytic activity of a PPR dynamics.

Another possible actor of these mechanism is neuropeptide FF (NPFF). Although this neuropeptide is more closely associated to nociception [116], its importance has been recently highlighted in mood disorders, particularly anxiety, related to withdrawal of drug addiction [117-120]. While drug withdrawal induces an anxiogenic mechanism through NPFF, the promise of a next, forthcoming drug intervention, as occurring in a PPR consultancy, might be read as an antagonist of NPFF-related mechanism, eliciting an NPY-mediated anxiolysis, as NPY ligands are able to interact with NPFF receptors [121]. The neuro-physiological circuit of this mechanism, whether or not inducing a placebo response, needs however further investigation.

From a neurophysiological point of view, placebo is a puzzling concept that should come from the complex consideration of how the brain-gut-immune axis works, as it is finely regulated by many of these neuropeptides [122, 123]. Therefore, while meeting the practitioner, the patient bears a stressful attitude in a PPR and only that circumstance may elicit an anxiolytic effect. Recent reports have elucidated that anxiolysis may be the result of a neuropetide/immune circuit that, while improving immune defense mechanisms, generate down-regulatory processes due to sedative stimuli (environment, sounds, light, practitioner's attitude and behaviour, and so on) or more generally defence mechanism to stress and anxiety. Although stressing situations may induce a strong, efficacious immune response, wellbeing, which is a classical symptom of placebo, results from the recovery of an immune homeostasis leading to a stress response even with coping and resilience mechanisms, and this should include necessarily a tolerance/down regulatory state after having responded efficaciously to the immune stressing stimulus and may involve even brain glia [124]. Although this would not mean healing at all, yet it is a classical mechanism of a placebo response. This mechanism is all but a on/off process but most probably is at a bifurcation point of a chaotic dynamics where the subject may sense a nocebo instead of a placebo process as a constant possibility during all the consultation, unless a series of "confirmatory" signals enforce the good perception of the patient in a PPR context.

3.3. Placebo as a Response to the Awareness of a Promising Result, Response to Stressful Events and Coping Mechanism

According to the hypothesis addressed above, mechanism eliciting a placebo response might involve an early anxiolytic, sedative action and this mechanism is the neuro-endogenous result of a stressing experience (e.g., meeting the practitioner, doubts on that friend's ability in giving the most proper advice and so on), which should trigger the immune machinery, a fact that may lead the individual to solve "spontaneously" his ailment, due to mechanisms ruled by endogenous neuropeptides on immunity ad inflammation, therefore showing a placebo response. The anxiolytic phase, as tentatively addressed above, should promote cognitive behaviours and defence mechanisms such as rationalization. The emotional forecasting to know what one wants to know, is a complex psychological mechanism including coping and resilience events, which may affect immune responses [125, 126]. In coping mechanism it is possible to suggest that the subject is prompted to address a stress-preventive attitude, an "optimism", particularly if the anxiolytic event takes place [127]. Recent reports have shown that a stressful experience accentuated acquired immunity particularly in optimists [128]. Optimism is therefore that particular attitude to acknowledge *what is coming as a promising therapy* just as *promising*. This attitude, anyway, might be mainly dependent on the PPR impact on the interviewed subject. Most probably, both psychological and immune stressors should act in a synergistic fashion in order to promote inflammation and sickness behaviour in humans [129]. This would mean that just meeting or approaching to meet the consulting member within a PPR dynamics might generate stress that in turn activates a complex mechanism of defence, hence affecting immunity. And actually, if a person undergoes drug intake by alone, a possible placebo effect should be attributed only to the awareness coming from the undeniable assurance that *such drug actually works.* Brydon and coworkers suggested therefore that the immune response works better if stress occurs in optimist people [129]. This pathway might hence include the possibility of a placebo response. Peripheral inflammatory events fundamentally influence central nervous system and mood-emotional responses [130]. Interestingly, effective coping strategies build resilience against stress-induced pathology and stress-mediated immune response. In this mechanism, NPY appears to play a major role [131]. As coping and other defence mechanisms to stress closely depend on the different individual personality, a main concern is if the placebo effect should depend on the particular patient who one is interviewing in a PPR [132]. Aside from fundamental differences in sex, age and genome array, the neuro-endocrine physiological axis with immunity depends on how the homeostatic machinery bridging metabolism and immune function actually works and how this complex dynamics depends on the individual genomic imprinting of gut microflora [133-135]. In this context an important role appears to be played by neuropeptide W [136-137]. From a neuro-physiological point of view, NPY has been recently implicated in the pathophysiology of certain mood disorders, including depression and anxiety. In particular, the deletion of NPY Y2 receptors in mice, resulted in enhanced NPY, GABA and glutamate release in specific brain areas linked to anxiety and stress-related behaviour such as the amygdala [138]. NPY is therefore a possible key factor in the neurophysiology of anxiety and stress and NPY receptors down-regulation a main mechanism related to anxiolysis and coping to stressing experiences. Furthermore, NPY is involved in adaptive emotional response following stress [139]. To date it is yet very difficult to elucidate which kind of molecular mechanism mediates patient's response to stress during a consultancy interview in a PPR context, probably NPY is a candidate. NPY is able to modulate cardiovascular function [140] and metabolic control [141]. Hypothesizing that in PPR the practitioner may exert a pro-sedation action, the role of NPY is mediated by the sedation-modulatory activity of the different Y1 and Y2 (but not Y5) NPY receptors [142], yet a polymorphism exists for Y1 and Y2 in general population, making particularly puzzling the neuro-physiological role of post-stress sedation in the onset of a placebo mechanism [143, 144]; NPY increases sedation induced by different anxiolytic events through Y1 receptors in the posterior hypothalamic area [145]. This is a well recognized region where critical stressing decisions, such as "fight or flight"are regulated and involve orexins [146]. Leptin and NPY are closely related [147, 148] and as leptin is involved in the modulation of the immune response [149], the gut/neuronal axis takes into account response to stress, sedation and immune response at a more systemic level, inducing a possible wellbeing signal through a leptin-axis, which in few words makes people satisfied as when they have eaten a meal [150, 151]. Although this may appear a speculative hypothesis, a placebo response may be attributed particularly to this mechanism, while the activity of leptin may modulate the gut/white adipose tissue (WAT) immune balance and promote WAT pro-inflammation.

The onset of a placebo mechanism in this PCDME process should involve a stress-defence action in which NPY, with other downstream hormones (cortisol, oxytocin, prolactin), peripheral neuropeptides (substance P) and orexins (leptin) might play a major role.

3.4. May Convinction about the Positive Outcome of a Therapy Induce a Placebo Response in a PPR or HEIAR Context?

The placebo effect may occurr also in orthodox therapy, when a patient is taking a pill for which *he is absolutely sure of the related positive effect on health.* The neurophysiology of conviction or trust is highly complex, involves rationalization and logical mental processes and appears much less influenced by emotional attitudes and responses linked to the previous described neuro/gut axis. Nevertheless, even this PCDME stage towards a placebo effect should account on a complex neuro-peptidergic system. This stage should pertain to brain (*neocortex*) activity, if we are disposed to consider every previous emotional activity more closely related to unconscious (brain/gut/immunity) neural processes [152]. To achieve a full awareness of the potential benefit associated with the treatment, a complex dynamics of unconscious and visual conscious events must take place to build up a trust and a conviction in the patient towards his/her practitioner. However, a possible boundary between these two conditions, namely conscious and unconscious, is difficult to describe [153]. Some well known hormones, such as oxytocin, might be implicated in the trust mechanism associated to PCDME, through the promotion of a social cognition attitude [154, 155]. The role of oxytocin is intriguing even in the neurophysiology of NPY. From an neuro-anatomical point of view the supraoctic nuclei, innervated by A1 neurons from the caudal ventro-lateral medulla, include substances co-localized in A1 termini, such as substance P, ATP, norepinephrine and NPY and particularly for ATP and the neuropeptide Y, a rapid and sustained stimulation of vasopressin and oxytocin have been observed [156]. Oxytocin has been recently associated to important neuro-psychic mechanisms leading to the ability in social interaction and cognitive processing of other's emotions [157, 158]. Oxytocin should act at the amygdale level interacting with ERK-mediated signaling to restore cognitive and social interaction deficit [159]. Furthermore, oxytocin plays a fundamental role in immune response and wound repair. At least in animal models, gut resident bacteria, which are triggered by oxytocin, are able to activate host CD4+Foxp3+ CD25+ immune T regulatory cells conveying transplantable wound healing capacity to naive Rag2-deficient animals [160]. This bulk of results should suggest that oxytocin might be involved as a fundamental factor of a placebo-induced response not only in a PPR but even in a HEIAR context. Oxytocin has a neurotropic anti-stress activity [161] and regulates many NPY-mediated activities, particularly those related to the metabolic/energetic balance [162]. During group meditation practices, it is arguable that oxytocin might mediate wellbeing by modulating anti-stress response and cardiovascular function in a "positive" social-interaction context [163-165]. A comparable condition may be generated in a good, polite, safe, empathic and comfortable PPR approach. However, as in the case of genetic polymorphism associated to NPY receptors, wide differences in the social behaviour, coping, response to stress are mediated by polymorphism in the oxytocin receptor (OXTR) gene [166-167]. Oxytocin exerts an important role on immune homeostasis, tolerance and regulation, as it was shown even in thymic epithelial cells [168-171] and therefore its role in a placebo-mediated mechanism should not be excluded, particularly for its promotion of a positive social interaction [172, 173], although the effect of oxytocin depends on the psychological attitude of the recruited/interviewed subject and on his attachment style [174] and should not be related to the empathic-driving neurological circuit triggered by MDMA [175]. In addition, oxytocin is involved in those mechanisms shaping awareness and memory, what we suggested to enforce own trust on the remedy and its effectiveness as recommended by the practitioner. Recent reports have highlighted that an important effect of oxytocin might be associated with enhanced responses and functional connectivity in emotional memory and reward processing neuronal regions [176]. In this perspective, a placebo response may involve oxytocin as a hormonal, neuro-active peptide to elicit immune regulation in the brain/gut/immune axis, leading to wellbeing and positive awareness of the consulting environment. The same molecule might be involved in any placebo-like effect due to emotional memory, as it may occur when an individual is taking a therapy that he trusts it *surely works*, assurance that is borne by social interactions [177].

In conclusion, although the neuro-physiological mechanism leading to a placebo response is yet far to be fully understood, many fundamental neurotropic molecules, able to act on the brain/gut/immune axis, affect social interaction, stress response, coping and resilience to stress, memory and reward mechanisms and placebo should pertain to this complex homeodynamics as a perceived effect of wellbeing. This effect may therefore come from a neuro-peptidergic and hormonal network, which is working to make the brain informed that the dynamics is going to balance, probably within the chaotic mechanism of strange attractors and bifurcations [178-183].

4. Placebo in Pharmacology and Medicine: Ethical Implications

4.1. Background

Which is the ethical implication of a placebo-related therapy? In evidence-based medicine, orthodox clinics and official therapy, placebo is exclusively used in palliative care but ethical concerns have raised by many authors about the use of CAM and homeopathy in recent years, as a "fake therapy hiding a placebo response", for which an ensuing debate was expanded [63, 64, 184-187]. Notwithstanding, it is very difficult to assess if an homeopathic remedy or a CAM-related approach works exclusively through a placebo effect. In this text, the many attempts to highlight if a PPR context may elicit a placebo response, have suggested that a complex dynamical network of neuropeptides and hormones might trigger a placebo mechanism in a supposed PCDME mechanism (see above). However, a placebo-related bioethical issue should pertain to those experimental studies and clinical trials in homeopathy whose results are claimed as promising for human health, therapy and healing. This promising attitude may generate positive expectation, trust and memory/reward mechanisms on the only PPR based approach, then generating a placebo response, successful immune reactivity and bias in interpretating clinical outcomes. To date we have no possibility to discriminate accurately wheat and chaffs in the use of CAM and homeopathy and evaluate a placebo effect respect to a real, quantifiable pharmacological action. The study of possible bias in homeopathy may help to foresee usefulness of this medical approach and contribute to an ethical evaluation of this practice.

4.2. Bias and Placebo: May People Be Innocently Deceived?

Experimental papers on the effect of homeopathic remedies may contain several biases and therefore induce people to believe that those remedies *surely successfully work* [188-192]. Big Pharma in the homeopathy market is prompted to create trust in people about the efficacy of their remedies, often with big claim and animated disputes [193, 194]. Expectations related to CAM and homeopathy could account on two main hallmarks, namely absence of side (adverse) effects and a personalized medicine approach. Interestingly, these two approaches should prevent an anxiogenic behaviour and the only possible anxiety-driving question is *shall I feel better with this remedy?* Actually, the relationship patient-practitioner (PPR), a fundamental in the bioethics of health care, has been promoted to the rank of a pharmacological mechanism and in this perspective it was generally defined as an inducer of an almost surely occurring “placebo effect”. Notwithstanding, placebo is a cumbersome issue because there is no way to demonstrate its existence beyond an implausible positive outcome within the PPR context. This consideration may raise criticism about the language and the meaning with which both RCTs and related meta-analysis reports were discussed, as trials employing placebos. Furthermore, the placebo effect needs therapeutics to be as much comprehensible as possible, in order to reduce any other component disturbance, such as possible nocebo effects due to the awareness of substance toxicity or inefficacy and to limit its effectiveness only on the relationship with the practitioner. During consultation, the illusory promise of a real effectiveness is potentially deceiving the patient because of the prejudice around the consideration that homeopathy is utterly implausible. In this respect, the practitioner who is prescribing a “low potency” homeopathic remedy to the patient, can express his conviction on a pharmacological basis, yet not too far from the herbal medicine approach. In most cases, positive outcome may derive from the consultation process rather to the homeopathic remedy, as previously indicated [195]. Therefore, a different bioethical consensus panel could be arranged during PPR, depending on the practitioner’s awareness about the content of the homeopathic medicine. Depending on the education level and beliefs of the practitioner, his attitude towards the patient will depend on her/his conviction and the “potency” (namely the association between the dilution factor and mechanical stress) of the homeopathic remedy. A positive psychological impact involves both the practitioner and patient only when homeopathic medicine deserves a certain “magnificent shyness” about its function, which lays on the exclusive foundation of homeopaths’ claims and debates and interestingly increases with the “complexity” of the remedy formulation, a field where positive expectations do not include any nocebo mechanism. This is more likely to be arguable for highest rather than lowest diluted remedies. In few words, there is apparently no way to demonstrate to date if a positive outcome from a high diluted (higher than 9cH or 15cH) homeopathic medicine arises either from a bio-molecular, bio-physical effect attributed to the same or to a placebo-induced mechanism. In this sense, the many RCTs did non help to confirm this thesis. On the other hand, placebo as control is biased by a large amount of chaotic and unpredictable effects that cannot be directly attributed to any neuro-immuno-endocrine mechanism causing a real placebo mechanism. In this perspective, the only truth appears to be that both patients and practitioners are yet groping in the dark.

This fashion to arrange the way by which people are informed about remedies excludes *a priori* the occurrence of a nocebo effect, as homeopathic remedies are deprived of potential adverse effects and can only offer wellbeing. The bioethical concern about the legitimacy of the proposal made by the practitioner towards the patient when homeopathy is taken into account, is largely hampered by the existence of many puzzling, unresolved and obscure issues, where the simple and honest truth about homeopathy might destroy its effect based on a supposed placebo mechanism. Interestingly, of about 4790 reports retrieved at the MESH term "homeopathy" in the Medline/Pubmed database, more than 90% are represented by comments, surveys, reviews and perspective papers aimed at convincing the reader about the goodness of homeopathy and more than 94.5% were published in niche journal on the CAM field, surely, an informative bias. This scenario should generate expectations and placebo as well, but very few evidence yet supports the possibility that CAM and homeopathy do not work exclusively through a placebo response.

4.3. Ethical Issues and Anthropology: Conclusion Remarks

It is clear that one cannot sustain, at the same time, the very low presence of a certain active substance within the homeopathic medicine and its presumptive ability to work in a pharmaceutical fashion, at least in the restricted horizon of the ability to comprehend largely exhibited by common people. People did not know or people were not made properly aware of the simple, honest fact that homeopathy might be only fresh water or simple sugar globules, in a strictly chemical sense, when accepting to use any homeopathic medicine to solve their health problems; anyway, even when they met a thorough awareness of this, they find very hard to trust this consideration, because they are prompted to believe that may be only a prejudice on their own. Therefore, what yet they believe to?

Some individuals are greatly disappointed from an insuccess occurred in official medicine while trying to heal them but many other are attracted by "soft and natural" therapeutics: these considerations may provide strong reasons to accept homeopathy or complementary and alternative medicine (CAM), hence a placebo-inducing therapy, as a valuable alternative in healthcare. In most of cases, people go to the practitioner and welcome homeopathy because they have a "positive prejudice" on that practice, They do not seem to care about some "jinxes" claiming that "homeopathy is utterly implausible". Actually homeopathic preparations are so thoroughly diluted into water or water/alcohol solvent, that, according to most opinions, they contain no significant amounts of active ingredients, hence they can have no therapeutic effects on the patient's body. Since now, despite a large number of studies having been declared to be conducted with success, there is no convincing evidence to support claims of effectiveness for homeopathy [184]. Yet, many people deceived themselves about the contrary. The fact may depend on many anthropological, cultural and psychological causes, e.g. that people are strongly attracted by an ideal come back to a wild and genuine nature-derived lifestyle, without evil and illness. The great bulk of homeopathic medicine comes from plants or organic sources, most of which characterized by toxic or even poisonous compounds. The Mithridates' myth to heal oneself by assuming a mirror, diluted and therefore harmless enemy, belongs to those everlasting legends built around the man and its fortune: therefore, as like as many other legends, it is hard to die. The same "similitude law" [196], in few words, has made up the puzzling hypothesis that a potentially adverse compound, mimicking the causative agent of a determined pathology, if highly diluted to prevent adverse effects, may restore health and successfully heal the patient. One is fighting against his enemy with the same weapons: this is amazing for most of people. Has this assumption a scientific tenet? The similitude law is funded on the the so-called provings. However, when a query on the MESH term "proving & homeopathy" in the Medline/Pubmed database is made, it allows to retrieve only 46/4789 results, i.e. 0.96%, very next to "none"; furthermore, the distribution of these terms throughout more than 60 years of Pubmed reporting in literature, elicited none or only one result for many long years and no more than 4-6 papers/year in the period 2004-2007. This somewhat awkward evidence could suggest to readers that similitude laws lay their foundations only on the traditional medicine born during C.H.S. Hahnemann's life and that homeopaths lay their prescription on the basis of a *Materia Medica* written in the nineteenth century, an edition which never has been experimentally reviewed by reappraised and rigorous "provings", at least as emerging from the current scientific literature [61, 197]. People cannot know, obviously, the existence of a Materia Medica Handbook or its further review, somehow or other. Therefore they simply trust the physician who simply trust homeopathy. They trust without being correctly informed, in few words. people are anthropologically bewitched by whatsoever occurs as a minority outcry. A modern society funded on civil rights, more than civil duties, awaits for anyone can fulfil his expectation, even when most of people should express a forthright disagreement. The misunderstanding pertains exclusively to cultural beliefs. Thinking according to the majority might be considered not merely a mature standpoint of the modern civilization but a hallmark of the ethical, financial or political establishment, which, in turn, is prompted to limit one's own freedom. This behaviour, and a more general opinion about, is built by people being informed collectively through press and mass media such as internet and by too expanded debates involving non experts, who often express their opinions on personal convictions and generally accepted points of view, not necessarily based on the scientific ground. In a scanty populated or quite desert field of experimental and clinical evidence, amounting to less than 1.0%, homeopathy addresses its strength on being a neglected minority within medical science, thus eliciting people to take up arms for freedom, i.e. freedom of health care, freedom of scientific investigation. Most of the crowded debates within homeopathy are related to these facts and considerations. Homeopathy stakes most of its success on modern people's anthropological attitude. Sugar globules sustain indirectly the expectation of a soft, sweet, natural medicine, a specular transposition of the same idea of health. The brief message is that while taking harmless sugar to care yourself, sugar that contain the promise of a recovery, you are merely taking a bright hope on you, you are taking merely the simple expectation to solve your trouble. The psychological landscape appears to be the only ground on which people make their decision about health when information is shallow and has a major role during a dramatic challenge with the so-called "last chance". The placebo mechanism, aside from any neuro-physiological fundamentals, feeds of these issues. As a consequence, people are rarely inclined to accept a polite, thorough and refined overview of the problem and its related solutions, involving science, when they are holding on tightly in defeating their rights, especially if concerning health, life, death and free thinking. Critical debates create doubts and increase weakness in a presumptive placebo mechanism. Broadly speaking this is an ethical standpoint to restart for the building of a constructive debate but it needs fundamentally that scientific research gives its answer without shallow and slovenly attempts and that press be more cautious in maddening a civil discussion. This asks for a deep renewal in the way with which the scientific debate about homeopathy must be expanded to public and how the concept of placebo is currently addressed in the field.

Correct information about the nature of homeopathic medicine deserves, therefore, particular attention. While the suggestion to describe a synthetic, summarizing pathway to the final product on labelling is a possible solution [198, 199], this finds much criticism among homeopaths, who claim the respect to the traditional Hahnemann's procedure but a more convincing reason of their disagreement could be the impact of labelling on the placebo effect. Furthermore, homeopathic medicine want not to be considered a subgroup of herbal medicine but most of practitioners do not succeed in distinguishing each other during their expertise and consultation. These facts lead to the conclusion that homeopathic medicine are not clearly identified on the ground of health practice and, in this sense, behave likewise illegal immigrants in a foreign country, an issue that raises bioethical concern and asks for an urgent thorough review by experts and politicians.

However, the concept of placebo may be yet considered in palliative medicine and trials, at least in theory, although criticism and doubts are frequently raised even in this field [200, 201]. An interesting debate is expanding about the use of placebo in clinics [202-204] but conclusions did not yet lead to any defined consensus panel or guideline. Treating a patient with a placebo is mostly considered as an unethical practice because the placebo effect should be restricted to the PPR mechanism and treatment might save its pharmacological, chemical nature, noone is obliged to use a sham medicine, unless therapy proved to be toxic or noxious if continually prescribed. Therefore, from an ethical point of view, the placebo issue yet pertains quite exclusively to homeopathy, at least to date, as in palliative care placebo is used in a larger context, where patients are simply helped to face at their dramatic problem. A more profound aid coming from the PPR context, the psychological environment to help the patient, characterizes palliative care respect to the anamnestic thorough profile performed in a PPR by CAM and homeopathy.

Anyway, many further insights are needed to elucidate the neuro-physiological mechanism underlying the placebo response. Placebo is a very good target to achieve during a therapeutical practice but its onset depends on a huge bulk of complex functions in the brain/gut/immune axis and on individual genetic polymorphism for many neuropeptide receptors, a circumstance that may discourage researchers when arranged some model to elucidate the neurophysiology of placebo. Placebo may help people to cope with their illness but stress-dependent reactions move their brain/gut/immune axis to recovery an homeostatic equilibrium: therefore, placebo should be induced to create an "optimistic" perspective to which one's own stress response is really efficacious. People needs sound, trustworthy "things" on which lay their own expectation, either a very good reputation of practitioner or the undoubtedly therapeutic efficacy of the prescribed therapy. Placebo should pertain to a dialogic psychological mechanism but actually it comes from complex biological phenomena involving endogenous neuropeptides, the brain/gut/immune axis, orexins, hormones and cytokines and in this sense any particular apparently negligible environmental factor might bear an important meaning in eliciting a placebo response.

In the next future, neuroscience may develop models, hypothesis and experimental planning which will shed a light on this mechanism and give a further fundamental aid on medical consultancy and therapy.

References

[1] Linde K, Clausius N, Ramirez G, Melchart D, Eitel F, Hedges LV, Jonas WB. Are the clinical effects of homeopathy placebo effects? A meta-analysis of placebo-controlled trials. *Lancet.* 1997 Sep 20;350(9081):834-43.

[2] Garattini S, Bertelé V, Banzi R. Placebo? no thanks, it might be bad for me! *Eur J Clin Pharmacol.* 2013 Mar;69(3):711-4.

[3] Garattini S, Bertele' V, Banzi R. Homeopathy cannot even be used to replace placebo. *Eur J Intern Med.* 2014 Jun;25(5):e68.

[4] Walach H. Does a highly diluted homoeopathic drug act as a placebo in healthy volunteers? Experimental study of Belladonna 30C in double-blind crossover design--a pilot study. *J Psychosom Res.* 1993 Dec;37(8):851-60.

[5] Kelley JM, Lembo AJ, Ablon JS, Villanueva JJ, Conboy LA, Levy R, Marci CD, Kerr CE, Kirsch I, Jacobson EE, Riess H, Kaptchuk TJ. Patient and practitioner influences on the placebo effect in irritable bowel syndrome. *Psychosom Med.* 2009 Sep;71(7):789-97.

[6] Kaptchuk TJ, Kelley JM, Conboy LA, Davis RB, Kerr CE, Jacobson EE, Kirsch I, Schyner RN, Nam BH, Nguyen LT, Park M, Rivers AL, McManus C, Kokkotou E, Drossman DA, Goldman P, Lembo AJ. Components of placebo effect: randomised controlled trial in patients with irritable bowel syndrome. *BMJ.* 2008 May 3;336(7651):999-1003.

[7] Kaptchuk TJ, Friedlander E, Kelley JM, Sanchez MN, Kokkotou E, Singer JP, Kowalczykowski M, Miller FG, Kirsch I, Lembo AJ.

Placebos without deception: a randomized controlled trial in irritable bowel syndrome. *PLoS One.* 2010 Dec 22;5(12):e15591.

[8] Peckham EJ, Nelson EA, Greenhalgh J, Cooper K, Roberts ER, Agrawal A. Homeopathy for treatment of irritable bowel syndrome. *Cochrane Database Syst Rev.* 2013 Nov 13;11:CD009710.

[9] Vickers AJ. Clinical trials of homeopathy and placebo: analysis of a scientific debate. *J Altern Complement Med.* 2000 Feb;6(1):49-56.

[10] Van Wassenhoven M. Priorities and methods for developing the evidence profile of homeopathy. Recommendations of the ECH general assembly and XVIII Symposium of GIRI. *Homeopathy.* 2005 Apr;94(2):107-24.

[11] Mathie RT. The research evidence base for homeopathy: a fresh assessment of the literature. *Homeopathy.* 2003 Apr;92(2):84-91.

[12] Milgrom LR. Is homeopathy possible? *J R Soc Promot Health.* 2006 Sep;126(5):211-8.

[13] Bellavite P, Marzotto M, Olioso D, Moratti E, Conforti A. High-dilution effects revisited. 2. Pharmacodynamic mechanisms. *Homeopathy.* 2014 Jan;103(1):22-43.

[14] Bellavite P, Marzotto M, Olioso D, Moratti E, Conforti A. High-dilution effects revisited. 1. Physicochemical aspects. *Homeopathy.* 2014 Jan;103(1):4-21.

[15] Milgrom LR. Patient-Practitioner-Remedy (PPR) Entanglement, Part 7: a gyroscopic metaphor for the vital force and its use to illustrate some of the empirical laws of homeopathy. *Forsch Komplementarmed Klass Naturheilkd.* 2004 Aug;11(4):212-23.

[16] Milgrom LR. Entanglement, knowledge, and their possible effects on the outcomes of blinded trials of homeopathic provings. *J Altern Complement Med.* 2006 Apr;12(3):271-9.

[17] Bellavite P, Pitari G, Italiano M. Homeopathy and placebo. *Homeopathy.* 2006 Jan;95(1):51.

[18] Ernst E. Homeopathy: what does the "best" evidence tell us? *Med J Aust.* 2010 Apr 19;192(8):458-60.

[19] Jonas WB, Kaptchuk TJ, Linde K. A critical overview of homeopathy. *Ann Intern Med.* 2003 Mar 4;138(5):393-9.

[20] Jütte R. Hahnemann and placebo. *Homeopathy.* 2014 Jul;103(3):208-12.

[21] Hahnemann S. *Reine Arzneimittellehre.* 1816, Dresden: Arnold.

[22] Dean ME. 'An innocent deception': placebo controls in the St Petersburg homeopathy trial, 1829-1830. *J R Soc Med.* 2006 Jul;99(7):375-6.

[23] Jütte R. The early history of the placebo. *Complement Ther Med.* 2013 Apr;21(2):94-7.
[24] Czerniak E, Davidson M. Placebo, a historical perspective. *Eur Neuropsychopharmacol.* 2012 Nov;22(11):770-4.
[25] Kerr CE, Milne I, Kaptchuk TJ. William Cullen and a missing mind-body link in the early history of placebos. *J R Soc Med.* 2008 Feb;101(2):89-92.
[26] Dean ME. A homeopathic origin for placebo controls: 'an invaluable gift of God'. *Altern Ther Health Med.* 2000 Mar;6(2):58-66.
[27] Maehle AH. Drugs on trial: experimental pharmacology and therapeutic innovation in the eighteenth century. *Clio Med.* 1999;53:1-376. Drugs on trial: experimental pharmacology and therapeutic innovation in the eighteenth century, Clio Medica 53, Wellcome Institute Series in the History of Medicine, Amsterdam and Atlanta, Rodopi, 1999, pp. 378.
[28] Huxtable RJ. A brief history of pharmacology, therapeutics and scientific thought. *Proc West Pharmacol Soc.* 1999;42:181-223.
[29] Hahnemann S. Heilart des jetzt herrschenden Nerven- oder Spitalfiebers (1814). In: Schmidt JM, Kaiser D (eds*). Kleine Medizinische Schriften.* Stuttgart: Karl F. Haug Verlag, 2001, pp 648e650..
[30] Hahnemann S. Transl. by Hempel CJ. *The Chronic Diseases,* Vol 1. New York: Wm. Radde, 1845. 165 note..
[31] Raicek JE, Stone BH, Kaptchuk TJ. Placebos in 19th century medicine: a quantitative analysis of the BMJ. *BMJ.* 2012 Dec 18;345:e8326.
[32] West RU. On the propriety of dispensing medicines. BMJ 1849;0:391.
[33] Tognotti E. The origins of the health defence system against contagious illness: the strategies of isolation and quarantine in Mediterranean cities from the XIV-XIX centuries. *Adler Mus Bull.* 2005;31(1):6-17.
[34] Brockow T, Franke A, Resch KL. [Is homeopathy more than a placebo?]. *Praxis* (Bern 1994). 1998 Dec 3;87(49):1687-94.
[35] Slabaugh WH. *Determination of Avogadro's number by Perrin's law J Chem Educ* 1965 42(9):471.
[36] Furiò CS, Azcona R, Guisasola J, Ratcliffe M. Difficulties in teaching the concepts of 'amount of substance' and 'mole'. *Int J Sci Educ* 2000; 22(12):1285-1304.
[37] Fang S.C, Hart C, Clarke D. Unpacking the Meaning of the Mole Concept for Secondary School Teachers and Students. *J. Chem. Educ.* 2014, 91, 351−356..
[38] Barański A . The Atomic Mass Unit, the Avogadro Constant, and the Mole: A Way To Understanding. *J. Chem. Educ.* 2012, 89, 97−102..

[39] Chirumbolo S. Molecules and nanoparticles in extreme homeopathic dilutions: is Avogadro's Constant a dogma? *Homeopathy.* 2011 Jul;100(3):107-8.

[40] Bellavite P, Marzotto M, Chirumbolo S, Conforti A. *Advances in homeopathy and immunology: a review of clinical research.* Front Biosci (Schol Ed). 2011 Jun 1;3:1363-89.

[41] Farhadi A, Bruninga K, Fields J, Keshavarzian A. Irritable bowel syndrome: an update on therapeutic modalities. *Expert Opin Investig Drugs.* 2001 Jul;10(7):1211-22.

[42] Chirumbolo S. Homeopathy against fulminant hepatic failure caused by fungal poisoning from the genus Amanita: Critical Comments. *The Ochsner Journal* 2014; 14:517.

[43] Dijkstra K, Pieterse M, Pruyn A. Physical environmental stimuli that turn healthcare facilities into healing environments through psychologically mediated effects: systematic review. *J Adv Nurs.* 2006 Oct;56(2):166-81.

[44] Irvine KN, Warber SL. Greening healthcare: practicing as if the natural environment really mattered. *Altern Ther Health Med.* 2002 Sep-Oct;8(5):76-83.

[45] Mathie RT, Lloyd SM, Legg LA, Clausen J, Moss S, Davidson JR, Ford I. Randomised placebo-controlled trials of individualised homeopathic treatment: systematic review and meta-analysis. *Syst Rev.* 2014 Dec 6;3(1):142..

[46] Haresnape C. An exploration of the relationship between placebo and homeopathy and the implications for clinical trial design. *JRSM Short Rep.* 2013 Jul 30;4(9):2042533313490927.

[47] Huang T, Shu X, Huang YS, Cheuk DK. Complementary and miscellaneous interventions for nocturnal enuresis in children. *Cochrane Database Syst Rev.*2011 Dec 7;(12):CD005230.

[48] Davidson JR, Crawford C, Ives JA, Jonas WB. Homeopathic treatments in psychiatry: a systematic review of randomized placebo-controlled studies. *J Clin Psychiatry.* 2011 Jun;72(6):795-805.

[49] Kassab S, Cummings M, Berkovitz S, van Haselen R, Fisher P. Homeopathic medicines for adverse effects of cancer treatments. *Cochrane Database Syst Rev.*2009 Apr 15;(2):CD004845.

[50] Lüdtke R, Rutten AL. The conclusions on the effectiveness of homeopathy highly depend on the set of analyzed trials. *J Clin Epidemiol.* 2008 Dec;61(12):1197-204.

[51] Relton C. Implications of the 'placebo effect' for CAM research. *Complement Ther Med.* 2013 Apr;21(2):121-4.

[52] Chirumbolo S. Randomized blinding in basic research of homeopathy: some comments. *Complement Ther Med.* 2011 Apr;19(2):107-8.

[53] Grogan S, Conner M, Norman P, Willits D, Porter I. Validation of a questionnaire measuring patient satisfaction with general practitioner services. *Qual Health Care*. 2000 Dec;9(4):210-5.

[54] Slort W, Schweitzer BP, Blankenstein AH, Abarshi EA, Riphagen II, Echteld MA, Aaronson NK, van der Horst H, Deliens L. Perceived barriers and facilitators for general practitioner-patient communication in palliative care: a systematic review. *Palliat Med.* 2011 Sep;25(6):613-29.

[55] Zanasi A, Mazzolini M, Tursi F, Morselli-Labate AM, Paccapelo A, Lecchi M.Homeopathic medicine for acute cough in upper respiratory tract infections and acute bronchitis: a randomized, double-blind, placebo-controlled trial. *Pulm Pharmacol Ther.* 2014 Feb;27(1):102-8.

[56] Adler UC, Krüger S, Teut M, Lüdtke R, Schützler L, Martins F, Willich SN, Linde K, Witt CM. Homeopathy for depression: a randomized, partially double-blind, placebo-controlled, four-armed study (DEP-HOM). *PLoS One.* 2013 Sep 23;8(9):e74537.

[57] Mathie RT, Hacke D, Clausen J, Nicolai T, Riley DS, Fisher P. Randomised controlled trials of homeopathy in humans: characterising the research journal literature for systematic review. *Homeopathy.* 2013 Jan;102(1):3-24.

[58] Sencer SF, Zhou T, Freedman LS, Ives JA, Chen Z, Wall D, Nieder ML, Grupp SA, Yu LC, Sahdev I, Jonas WB, Wallace JD, Oberbaum M. Traumeel S in preventing and treating mucositis in young patients undergoing SCT: a report of the Children's Oncology Group. *Bone Marrow Transplant.* 2012 Nov;47(11):1409-14.

[59] Paris A, Schmidlin S, Mouret S, Hodaj E, Marijnen P, Boujedaini N, Polosan M, Cracowski JL. Effect of Gelsemium 5CH and 15CH on anticipatory anxiety: a phase III, single-centre, randomized, placebo-controlled study. *Fundam Clin Pharmacol.* 2012 Dec;26(6):751-60.

[60] Macías-Cortés Edel C, Aguilar-Faisal L, Asbun-Bojalil J. Efficacy of individualized homeopathic treatment and fluoxetine for moderate to severe depression in peri- and postmenopausal women (HOMDEP-MENOP): study protocol for a randomized, double-dummy, double-blind, placebo-controlled trial. *Trials.* 2013 Apr 23;14:105.

[61] Brien S, Lewith G, Bryant T. Ultramolecular homeopathy has no observable clinical effects. A randomized, double-blind, placebo-controlled proving trial of Belladonna 30C. Br J Clin Pharmacol. 2003 Nov;56(5):562-8. Erratum in: *Br J Clin Pharmacol.* 2004 Jan;57(1):117.

[62] Weatherley-Jones E, Nicholl JP, Thomas KJ, Parry GJ, McKendrick MW, Green ST, Stanley PJ, Lynch SP. A randomised, controlled, triple-blind trial of the efficacy of homeopathic treatment for chronic fatigue syndrome. *J Psychosom Res.* 2004 Feb;56(2):189-97.

[63] Ernst E. Homeopathy, a "helpful placebo" or an unethical intervention? *Trends Pharmacol Sci.* 2010 Jan;31(1):1.

[64] Ross P. Homeopathy, a "helpful placebo"; or an unethical intervention? Edzard Ernst Reply. *Trends Pharmacol Sci.* 2010 Jul;31(7):297; author reply 297-8.

[65] Bennett P, Wilkinson S. A comparison of psychological and medical treatment of the irritable bowel syndrome. *Br J Clin Psychol.* 1985 Sep;24 (Pt 3):215-6.

[66] Sanders KA, Blanchard EB, Sykes MA. Preliminary study of a self-administered treatment for irritable bowel syndrome: comparison to a wait list control group. *Appl Psychophysiol Biofeedback.* 2007 Jun;32(2):111-9.

[67] Hariri AR, Bookheimer SY, Mazziotta JC. Modulating emotional responses: effects of a neocortical network on the limbic system. *Neuroreport.* 2000 Jan 17;11(1):43-8..

[68] Okon-Singer H, Hendler T, Pessoa L, Shackman AJ. Introduction to the special research topic on the neurobiology of emotion-cognition interactions. *Front HumNeurosci.* 2015 Jan 30;8:1051.

[69] Stein M, Keller SE, Schleifer SJ. Immune system. Relationship to anxiety disorders. *Psychiatr Clin North Am.* 1988 Jun;11(2):349-60.

[70] Stein M. Stress, depression, and the immune system. *J Clin Psychiatry.* 1989 May;50 Suppl:35-40; discussion 41-2.

[71] Fogarty LA, Curbow BA, Wingard JR, McDonnell K, Somerfield MR. Can 40 seconds of compassion reduce patient anxiety? *J Clin Oncol.* 1999 Jan;17(1):371-9.

[72] Graugaard PK, Eide H, Finset A. Interaction analysis of physician-patient communication: the influence of trait anxiety on communication and outcome. *Patient Educ Couns.* 2003 Feb;49(2):149-56.

[73] Zill JM, Christalle E, Müller E, Härter M, Dirmaier J, Scholl I. Measurement of physician-patient communication--a systematic review. *PLoS One.* 2014 Dec 22;9(12):e112637.

[74] Croicu C, Chwastiak L, Katon W. Approach to the patient with multiple somatic symptoms. *Med Clin North Am.* 2014 Sep;98(5):1079-95.

[75] Forsythe P, Kunze WA. Voices from within: gut microbes and the CNS. *Cell Mol Life Sci.* 2013 Jan;70(1):55-69.

[76] Irwin M, Patterson T, Smith TL, Caldwell C, Brown SA, Gillin JC, Grant I. Reduction of immune function in life stress and depression. *Biol Psychiatry.* 1990 Jan 1;27(1):22-30.

[77] Nautiyal KM, Ribeiro AC, Pfaff DW, Silver R. Brain mast cells link the immune system to anxiety-like behavior. *Proc Natl Acad Sci U S A.* 2008 Nov 18;105(46):18053-7.

[78] Lozano D, Gonzales-Portillo GS, Acosta S, de la Pena I, Tajiri N, Kaneko Y, Borlongan CV. Neuroinflammatory responses to traumatic brain injury: etiology, clinical consequences, and therapeutic opportunities. *Neuropsychiatr Dis Treat.*2015 Jan 8;11:97-106.

[79] Wohleb ES, McKim DB, Sheridan JF, Godbout JP. Monocyte trafficking to the brain with stress and inflammation: a novel axis of immune-to-brain communication that influences mood and behavior. *Front Neurosci.* 2015 Jan 21;8:447..

[80] Reader BF, Jarrett BL, McKim DB, Wohleb ES, Godbout JP, Sheridan JF.Peripheral and central effects of repeated social defeat stress: Monocyte trafficking, microglial activation, and anxiety. *Neuroscience.* 2015 Jan14;289C:429-442.

[81] Hardy RS, Raza K, Cooper MS. Endogenous glucocorticoids in inflammation:contributions of systemic and local responses. *Swiss Med Wkly.* 2012 Aug6;142:w13650.

[82] Ota Y, Ago Y, Tanaka T, Hasebe S, Toratani Y, Onaka Y, Hashimoto H, Takuma K, Matsuda T. Anxiolytic-like effects of restraint during the dark cycle in adolescent mice. *Behav Brain Res.* 2015 Feb 13. pii: S0166-4328(15)00087-X. doi:10.1016/j.bbr.2015.02.010.

[83] Zhu H, Mingler MK, McBride ML, Murphy AJ, Valenzuela DM, Yancopoulos GD, Williams MT, Vorhees CV, Rothenberg ME. Abnormal response to stress and impaired NPS-induced hyperlocomotion, anxiolytic effect and corticosterone increase in mice lacking NPSR1. *Psychoneuroendocrinology.* 2010 Sep;35(8):1119-32.

[84] Donner J, Haapakoski R, Ezer S, Melén E, Pirkola S, Gratacòs M, Zucchelli M, Anedda F, Johansson LE, Söderhäll C, Orsmark-Pietras C, Suvisaari J, Martín-Santos R, Torrens M, Silander K, Terwilliger JD, Wickman M, Pershagen G, Lönnqvist J, Peltonen L, Estivill X, D'Amato M, Kere J, Alenius H, Hovatta I. Assessment of the

neuropeptide S system in anxiety disorders. *Biol Psychiatry.*2010 Sep 1;68(5):474-83.

[85] Camilleri M, Carlson P, Zinsmeister AR, McKinzie S, Busciglio I, Burton D, Zucchelli M, D'Amato M. Neuropeptide S receptor induces neuropeptide expression and associates with intermediate phenotypes of functional gastrointestinal disorders. *Gastroenterology.* 2010 Jan;138(1):98-107.e4.

[86] Rizzi A, Vergura R, Marzola G, Ruzza C, Guerrini R, Salvadori S, Regoli D, Calo G. Neuropeptide S is a stimulatory anxiolytic agent: a behavioural study in mice. Br J Pharmacol. 2008 May;154(2):471-9.

[87] Reinscheid RK, Xu YL. Neuropeptide S as a novel arousal promoting peptide transmitter. FEBS J. 2005 Nov;272(22):5689-93.

[88] Okamura N, Reinscheid RK. Neuropeptide S: a novel modulator of stress and arousal. *Stress.* 2007 Aug;10(3):221-6.

[89] Jonker MA, Heneghan AF, Fechner JH, Pierre JF, Sano Y, Lan J, Kudsk KA. Gut Lymphocyte Phenotype Changes After Parenteral Nutrition and Neuropeptide Administration. *Ann Surg.* 2015 Jan 5, *in press*.

[90] Ren W, Kiritoshi T, Grégoire S, Ji G, Guerrini R, Calo G, Neugebauer V. Neuropeptide S: a novel regulator of pain-related amygdala plasticity and behaviors. *J Neurophysiol.* 2013 Oct;110(8):1765-81.

[91] Dine J, Ionescu IA, Stepan J, Yen YC, Holsboer F, Landgraf R, Eder M, Schmidt U. Identification of a role for the ventral hippocampus in neuropeptide S-elicited anxiolysis. *PLoS One.* 2013;8(3):e60219.

[92] Ionescu IA, Dine J, Yen YC, Buell DR, Herrmann L, Holsboer F, Eder M, Landgraf R, Schmidt U. Intranasally administered neuropeptide S (NPS) exerts anxiolytic effects following internalization into NPS receptor-expressing neurons. *Neuropsychopharmacology.* 2012 May;37(6):1323-37.

[93] Lotti T, D'Erme AM, Hercogová J. The role of neuropeptides in the control of regional immunity. *Clin Dermatol.* 2014 Sep-Oct;32(5):633-45.

[94] Yao Y, Su J, Yang G, Zhang G, Lei Z, Zhang F, Li X, Kou R, Liu Y, Liu J.Effects of neuropeptide S on the proliferation of splenic lymphocytes, phagocytosis, and proinflammatory cytokine production of pulmonary alveolar macrophages in the pig. *Peptides.* 2011 Jan;32(1):118-24.

[95] Farzi A, Reichmann F, Holzer P. The homeostatic role of neuropeptide Y in immune function and its impact on mood and behaviour. *Acta Physiol* (Oxf). 2015 Mar;213(3):603-27.

[96] Zukowska Z, Pons J, Lee EW, Li L. Neuropeptide Y: a new mediator linking sympathetic nerves, blood vessels and immune system? *Can J Physiol Pharmacol.*2003 Feb;81(2):89-94.

[97] Bedoui S, Kawamura N, Straub RH, Pabst R, Yamamura T, von Hörsten S. Relevance of neuropeptide Y for the neuroimmune crosstalk. *J Neuroimmunol.* 2003 Jan;134(1-2):1-11.

[98] Wheway J, Herzog H, Mackay F. NPY and receptors in immune and inflammatory diseases. *Curr Top Med Chem.* 2007;7(17):1743-52.

[99] Dimitrijević M, Stanojević S. The intriguing mission of neuropeptide Y in the immune system. *Amino Acids.* 2013 Jul;45(1):41-53.

[100] Buttari B, Profumo E, Domenici G, Tagliani A, Ippoliti F, Bonini S, Businaro R, Elenkov I, Riganò R. Neuropeptide Y induces potent migration of human immature dendritic cells and promotes a Th2 polarization. *FASEB J.* 2014 Jul;28(7):3038-49.

[101] Medeiros PJ, Al-Khazraji BK, Novielli NM, Postovit LM, Chambers AF, Jackson DN. Neuropeptide Y stimulates proliferation and migration in the 4T1 breast cancer cell line. *Int J Cancer.* 2012 Jul 15;131(2):276-86.

[102] Sheriff S, Ali M, Yahya A, Haider KH, Balasubramaniam A, Amlal H. Neuropeptide Y Y5 receptor promotes cell growth through extracellular signal-regulated kinase signaling and cyclic AMP inhibition in a human breast cancer cell line. *Mol Cancer Res.* 2010 Apr;8(4):604-14.

[103] Cohen H, Liu T, Kozlovsky N, Kaplan Z, Zohar J, Mathé AA. The neuropeptide Y (NPY)-ergic system is associated with behavioral resilience to stress exposure in an animal model of post-traumatic stress disorder. *Neuropsychopharmacology.* 2012 Jan;37(2):350-63.

[104] Heilig M, McLeod S, Brot M, Heinrichs SC, Menzaghi F, Koob GF, Britton KT.Anxiolytic-like action of neuropeptide Y: mediation by Y1 receptors in amygdala, and dissociation from food intake effects. *Neuropsychopharmacology.* 1993 Jun;8(4):357-63.

[105] Kask A, Nguyen HP, Pabst R, Von Hörsten S. Neuropeptide Y Y1 receptor-mediated anxiolysis in the dorsocaudal lateral septum: functional antagonism of corticotropin-releasing hormone-induced anxiety. *Neuroscience.*2001;104(3):799-806.

[106] Antonijevic IA, Murck H, Bohlhalter S, Frieboes RM, Holsboer F, Steiger A.Neuropeptide Y promotes sleep and inhibits ACTH and cortisol release in young men. *Neuropharmacology.* 2000 Jun 8;39(8):1474-81.

[107] Ohya T, Nagai T, Araki Y, Yanagawa T, Tanabe T, Iyoda K, Kurihara M, Yamamoto K, Masunaga K, Iizuka C, Nagamitsu S, Yamashita Y, Awaya Y, Maekawa K, Matsuishi T; Research Group on Adverse Effects of Vaccination in Patients with Neurological Disorders. A pilot study on the changes in immunity after ACTH therapy in patients with West syndrome. *Brain Dev.* 2009 Nov;31(10):739-43.

[108] Kask A, Harro J, von Hörsten S, Redrobe JP, Dumont Y, Quirion R. The neurocircuitry and receptor subtypes mediating anxiolytic-like effects of neuropeptide Y. *Neurosci Biobehav Rev.* 2002 May;26(3):259-83.

[109] Fulford AJ. Endogenous nociceptin system involvement in stress responses and anxiety behavior. *Vitam Horm.* 2015;97:267-93.

[110] Xie XS. The Neuronal Circuit Between Nociceptin/Orphanin FQ and Hypocretins/Orexins Coordinately Modulates Stress-Induced Analgesia and Anxiety-Related Behavior. *Vitam Horm.* 2015;97:295-321.

[111] Thompson AA, Liu W, Chun E, Katritch V, Wu H, Vardy E, Huang XP, Trapella C, Guerrini R, Calo G, Roth BL, Cherezov V, Stevens RC. Structure of the nociceptin/orphanin FQ receptor in complex with a peptide mimetic. *Nature.* 2012 May 16;485(7398):395-9.

[112] Gavioli EC, de Medeiros IU, Monteiro MC, Calo G, Romão PR. Nociceptin/Orphanin FQ-NOP Receptor System in Inflammatory and Immune-Mediated Diseases. *Vitam Horm.* 2015;97:241-66.

[113] Asth L, Correia N, Lobão-Soares B, De Lima TC, Guerrini R, Calo' G, Soares-Rachetti VP, Gavioli EC. Nociceptin/orphanin FQ induces simultaneously anxiolytic and amnesic effects in the mouse elevated T-maze task. *Naunyn Schmiedebergs Arch Pharmacol.* 2015 Jan;388(1):33-41.

[114] Vitale G, Arletti R, Ruggieri V, Cifani C, Massi M. Anxiolytic-like effects of nociceptin/orphanin FQ in the elevated plus maze and in the conditioned defensive burying test in rats. *Peptides.* 2006 Sep;27(9):2193-200.

[115] Mallimo EM, Kusnecov AW. The role of orphanin FQ/nociceptin in neuroplasticity: relationship to stress, anxiety and neuroinflammation. *Front Cell Neurosci.* 2013 Oct 8;7:173.

[116] Yang HY, Tao T, Iadarola MJ. Modulatory role of neuropeptide FF system in nociception and opiate analgesia. *Neuropeptides.* 2008 Feb;42(1):1-18.

[117] Kotlinska J, Pachuta A, Dylag T, Silberring J. Neuropeptide FF (NPFF) reduces the expression of morphine- but not of ethanol-induced

conditioned place preference in rats. *Peptides.* 2007 Nov;28(11):2235-42.

[118] Kotlinska J, Pachuta A, Silberring J. Neuropeptide FF (NPFF) reduces the expression of cocaine-induced conditioned place preference and cocaine-induced sensitization in animals. *Peptides.* 2008 Jun;29(6):933-9.

[119] Kotlinska J, Pachuta A, Bochenski M, Silberring J. Dansyl-PQRamide, a putative antagonist of NPFF receptors, reduces anxiety-like behavior of ethanol withdrawal in a plus-maze test in rats. *Peptides.* 2009 Jun;30(6):1165-72.

[120] Kotlinska JH, Gibula-Bruzda E, Koltunowska D, Raoof H, Suder P, Silberring J. Modulation of neuropeptide FF (NPFF) receptors influences the expression of amphetamine-induced conditioned place preference and amphetamine withdrawal anxiety-like behavior in rats. *Peptides.* 2012 Jan;33(1):156-63.

[121] Mollereau C, Gouardères C, Dumont Y, Kotani M, Detheux M, Doods H, Parmentier M, Quirion R, Zajac JM. Agonist and antagonist activities on human NPFF(2) receptors of the NPY ligands GR231118 and BIBP3226. *Br J Pharmacol.* 2001 May;133(1):1-4.

[122] Holzer P, Reichmann F, Farzi A. Neuropeptide Y, peptide YY and pancreatic polypeptide in the gut-brain axis. *Neuropeptides.* 2012 Dec;46(6):261-74.

[123] Holzer P, Farzi A. Neuropeptides and the microbiota-gut-brain axis. *Adv Exp Med Biol.* 2014;817:195-219.

[124] Dissel S, Seugnet L, Thimgan MS, Silverman N, Angadi V, Thacher PV, Burnham MM, Shaw PJ. Differential activation of immune factors in neurons and glia contribute to individual differences in resilience/vulnerability to sleep disruption. *Brain Behav Immun.* 2014 Oct 30. pii: S0889-1591(14)00472-3. doi: 10.1016/j.bbi.2014.09.019..

[125] Wilson TD and Gilbert DT, Affective forecasting-knowing what to want *Curr Direct Psycholog Sci* 205; 14(3):131-4.

[126] Biondi M, Pancheri P. *Depression and coping style as modulators of the immune response under stress in Stress and Immunity,* NP Plotnikoff, AJ Murgo, RE Faith, J Wybran eds, CRC Press, BocaRaton, FL, USA, 1991, p 189.

[127] Segerstrom SC, Taylor SE, Kemeny ME, Fahey JL. Optimism is associated with mood, coping, and immune change in response to stress. J Pers Soc Psychol. 1998 Jun;74(6):1646-55.

[128] Brydon L, Walker C, Wawrzyniak AJ, Chart H, Steptoe A. Dispositional optimism and stress-induced changes in immunity and negative mood. *Brain Behav Immun.* 2009 Aug;23(6):810-6.

[129] Brydon L, Walker C, Wawrzyniak A, Whitehead D, Okamura H, Yajima J, Tsuda A, Steptoe A. Synergistic effects of psychological and immune stressors on inflammatory cytokine and sickness responses in humans. *Brain Behav Immun.* 2009 Feb;23(2):217-24.

[130] Harrison NA, Brydon L, Walker C, Gray MA, Steptoe A, Dolan RJ, Critchley HD. Neural origins of human sickness in interoceptive responses to inflammation. *Biol Psychiatry.* 2009 Sep 1;66(5):415-22.

[131] Hawley DF, Bardi M, Everette AM, Higgins TJ, Tu KM, Kinsley CH, Lambert KG. Neurobiological constituents of active, passive, and variable coping strategies in rats: integration of regional brain neuropeptide Y levels and cardiovascular responses. *Stress.* 2010 Mar;13(2):172-83.

[132] Jakšić N, Aukst-Margetić B, Jakovljević M. Does personality play a relevant role in the placebo effect? *Psychiatr Danub.* 2013 Mar;25(1):17-23.

[133] Keightley PC, Koloski NA, Talley NJ. Pathways in gut-brain communication:Evidence for distinct gut-to-brain and brain-to-gut syndromes. *Aust N Z J Psychiatry.* 2015 Mar;49(3):207-214.

[134] Mayer EA, Tillisch K, Gupta A. Gut/brain axis and the microbiota. *J Clin Invest.* 2015 Feb 17. pii: 76304. doi: 10.1172/JCI76304.

[135] Stilling RM, Dinan TG, Cryan JF. Microbial genes, brain & behaviour - epigenetic regulation of the gut-brain axis. *Genes Brain Behav.* 2014 Jan;13(1):69-86.

[136] Takenoya F, Kageyama H, Shiba K, Date Y, Nakazato M, Shioda S. Neuropeptide W: a key player in the homeostatic regulation of feeding and energy metabolism? Ann N Y Acad Sci. 2010 Jul;1200:162-9.

[137] Hondo M, Ishii M, Sakurai T. The NPB/NPW neuropeptide system and its role in regulating energy homeostasis, pain, and emotion. *Results Probl Cell Differ.*2008;46:239-56.

[138] Tschenett A, Singewald N, Carli M, Balducci C, Salchner P, Vezzani A, Herzog H, Sperk G. Reduced anxiety and improved stress coping ability in mice lacking NPY-Y2 receptors. *Eur J Neurosci.* 2003 Jul;18(1):143-8.

[139] McGuire JL, Larke LE, Sallee FR, Herman JP, Sah R. Differential Regulation of Neuropeptide Y in the Amygdala and Prefrontal Cortex

during Recovery from Chronic Variable Stress. *Front Behav Neurosci.* 2011 Sep 15;5:54.

[140] Jacques D, Abdel-Samad D. Neuropeptide Y (NPY) and NPY receptors in the cardiovascular system: implication in the regulation of intracellular calcium.*Can J Physiol Pharmacol.* 2007 Jan;85(1):43-53.

[141] Singh RB, Pella D, Mechirova V, Otsuka K. Can brain dysfunction be a predisposing factor for metabolic syndrome? *Biomed Pharmacother.* 2004 Oct;58 Suppl 1:S56-68.

[142] Naveilhan P, Canals JM, Arenas E, Ernfors P. Distinct roles of the Y1 and Y2 receptors on neuropeptide Y-induced sensitization to sedation. *J Neurochem.* 2001 Sep;78(6):1201-7.

[143] Testa A, Mallamaci F, Macrì R, Pisano A, Spoto B, Malatino LS, Stancanelli B, Tripepi G, Benedetto FA, Zoccali C. Neuropeptide Y receptor Y2 gene polymorphism interacts with plasma neuropeptide Y levels in predicting left ventricular hypertrophy in dialysis patients. *J Hypertens.* 2010 Aug;28(8):1745-51.

[144] Ito H, Morita T, Suehiro T, Tahara K, Ikeda Y, Nakauchi Y, Makino S, Nishiya K, Hashimoto K. Neuropeptide Y Y1 receptor polymorphism as a prognostic predictor in Japanese patients with IgA nephropathy. *Clin Nephrol.* 1999 May;51(5):272-9.

[145] Naveilhan P, Canals JM, Valjakka A, Vartiainen J, Arenas E, Ernfors P.Neuropeptide Y alters sedation through a hypothalamic Y1-mediated mechanism. *Eur J Neurosci.* 2001 Jun;13(12):2241-6..

[146] Johnson PL, Molosh A, Fitz SD, Truitt WA, Shekhar A. Orexin, stress, and anxiety/panic states. *Prog Brain Res.* 2012;198:133-61.

[147] Kassab S, Abdul-Ghaffar T, Nagalla DS, Sachdeva U, Nayar U. Interactions between leptin, neuropeptide-Y and insulin with chronic diurnal fasting during Ramadan. *Ann Saudi Med.* 2004 Sep-Oct;24(5):345-9.

[148] Lee SJ, Verma S, Simonds SE, Kirigiti MA, Kievit P, Lindsley SR, Loche A, Smith MS, Cowley MA, Grove KL. Leptin stimulates neuropeptide Y and cocaine amphetamine-regulated transcript coexpressing neuronal activity in the dorsomedial hypothalamus in diet-induced obese mice. *J Neurosci.* 2013 Sep 18;33(38):15306-17.

[149] Blüher M, Mantzoros CS. From leptin to other adipokines in health and disease: facts and expectations at the beginning of the 21st century. *Metabolism.* 2015 Jan;64(1):131-45.

[150] Myers MG Jr, Münzberg H, Leinninger GM, Leshan RL. The geometry of leptin action in the brain: more complicated than a simple ARC. *Cell Metab.* 2009 Feb;9(2):117-23.

[151] Romon M, Lebel P, Velly C, Marecaux N, Fruchart JC, Dallongeville J. Leptin response to carbohydrate or fat meal and association with subsequent satiety and energy intake. *Am J Physiol.* 1999 Nov;277(5 Pt 1):E855-61.

[152] Schmid MC, Maier A. To see or not to see - Thalamo-cortical networks during blindsight and perceptual suppression. *Prog Neurobiol. 2015* Feb 7. pii:S0301-0082(15)00009-X. doi: 10.1016/j.pneurobio.2015.01.001.

[153] Brogaard B. Are there unconscious perceptual processes? *Conscious Cogn.* 2011 Jun;20(2):449-63.

[154] Kirsch P, Esslinger C, Chen Q, Mier D, Lis S, Siddhanti S, Gruppe H, Mattay VS, Gallhofer B, Meyer-Lindenberg A. Oxytocin modulates neural circuitry for social cognition and fear in humans. *J Neurosci.* 2005 Dec 7;25(49):11489-93.

[155] Baumgartner T, Heinrichs M, Vonlanthen A, Fischbacher U, Fehr E. Oxytocin shapes the neural circuitry of trust and trust adaptation in humans. *Neuron.* 2008 May 22;58(4):639-50.

[156] Kapoor JR, Sladek CD. Substance P and NPY differentially potentiate ATP and adrenergic stimulated vasopressin and oxytocin release. *Am J Physiol Regul Integr Comp Physiol.* 2001 Jan;280(1):R69-78.

[157] Colonnello V, Chen FS, Panksepp J, Heinrichs M. Oxytocin sharpens self-other perceptual boundary. *Psychoneuroendocrinology.* 2013 Dec;38(12):2996-3002.

[158] Ellingsen DM, Wessberg J, Chelnokova O, Olausson H, Laeng B, Leknes S. In touch with your emotions: oxytocin and touch change social impressions while others' facial expressions can alter touch. *Psychoneuroendocrinology.* 2014 Jan;39:11-20..

[159] Wang Y, Zhao S, Wu Z, Feng Y, Zhao C, Zhang C. Oxytocin involves in the regulation of social behaviors in medial amygdala-lesioned mice via inhibiting ERK signaling pathway. *Clin Exp Pharmacol Physiol.* 2015 Feb 24. doi:10.1111/1440-1681.12378.

[160] Poutahidis T, Kearney SM, Levkovich T, Qi P, Varian BJ, Lakritz JR, Ibrahim YM, Chatzigiagkos A, Alm EJ, Erdman SE. Microbial symbionts accelerate wound healing via the neuropeptide hormone oxytocin. *PLoS One.* 2013 Oct 30;8(10):e78898.

[161] Bali A, Singh N, Jaggi AS. Neuropeptides as therapeutic targets to combat stress-associated behavioral and neuroendocrinological effects. *CNS Neurol Disord Drug Targets.* 2014 Mar;13(2):347-68.

[162] Coiro V, Volpi R, Volta E, Magotti MG, Cataldo S, Stella A, Chiodera P. Systemic oxytocin administration modulates NPY response to insulin-induced hypoglycemia in man. *Horm Metab Res.* 2011 Feb;43(2):146-7.

[163] Uvnäs-Moberg K. Oxytocin linked antistress effects--the relaxation and growth response. *Acta Physiol Scand Suppl.* 1997;640:38-42.

[164] Uvnäs-Moberg K. Oxytocin may mediate the benefits of positive social interaction and emotions. *Psychoneuroendocrinology.* 1998 Nov;23(8):819-35.

[165] Uvnäs-Moberg K, Petersson M. [Oxytocin--biochemical link for human relations. Mediator of antistress, well-being, social interaction, growth, healing...]. *Lakartidningen.* 2004 Aug 26;101(35):2634-9.

[166] Haram M, Tesli M, Bettella F, Djurovic S, Andreassen OA, Melle I. Association between Genetic Variation in the Oxytocin Receptor Gene and Emotional Withdrawal, but not between Oxytocin Pathway Genes and Diagnosis in Psychotic Disorders. *Front Hum Neurosci.* 2015 Jan 23;9:9.

[167] Montag C, Brockmann EM, Bayerl M, Rujescu D, Müller DJ, Gallinat J. Oxytocin and oxytocin receptor gene polymorphisms and risk for schizophrenia: a case-control study. *World J Biol Psychiatry.* 2013 Sep;14(7):500-8.

[168] Pittman QJ. A neuro-endocrine-immune symphony. *J Neuroendocrinol.* 2011 Dec;23(12):1296-7.

[169] Carnio EC, Moreto V, Giusti-Paiva A, Antunes-Rodrigues J. Neuro-immune-endocrine mechanisms during septic shock: role for nitric oxide in vasopressin and oxytocin release. *Endocr Metab Immune Disord Drug Targets.* 2006 Jun;6(2):137-42.

[170] Wiemann M, Ehret G. Subcellular localization of immunoreactive oxytocin within thymic epithelial cells of the male mouse. *Cell Tissue Res.* 1993 Jul;273(1):79-87.

[171] Geenen V, Bodart G, Henry S, Michaux H, Dardenne O, Charlet-Renard C, Martens H, Hober D. Programming of neuroendocrine self in the thymus and its defect in the development of neuroendocrine autoimmunity. *Front Neurosci.* 2013 Oct 16;7:187.

[172] Preckel K, Scheele D, Kendrick KM, Maier W, Hurlemann R. Oxytocin facilitates social approach behavior in women. *Front Behav Neurosci.* 2014 May 27;8:191.

[173] Abu-Akel A, Palgi S, Klein E, Decety J, Shamay-Tsoory S. Oxytocin increases empathy to pain when adopting the other- but not the self-perspective. *Soc Neurosci.* 2015;10(1):7-15.

[174] Fang A, Hoge EA, Heinrichs M, Hofmann SG. Attachment Style Moderates the Effects of Oxytocin on Social Behaviors and Cognitions During Social Rejection: Applying an RDoC Framework to Social Anxiety. *Clin Psychol Sci.* 2014 Nov 1;2(6):740-747.

[175] Kuypers KP, de la Torre R, Farre M, Yubero-Lahoz S, Dziobek I, Van den Bos W, Ramaekers JG. No evidence that MDMA-induced enhancement of emotional empathy is related to peripheral oxytocin levels or 5-HT1a receptor activation. *PLoS One.* 2014 Jun 27;9(6):e100719.

[176] Hu J, Qi S, Becker B, Luo L, Gao S, Gong Q, Hurlemann R, Kendrick KM. Oxytocin selectively facilitates learning with social feedback and increases activity and functional connectivity in emotional memory and reward processing regions. *Hum Brain Mapp.* 2015 Feb 9. doi: 10.1002/hbm.22760.

[177] Gur R, Tendler A, Wagner S. Long-term social recognition memory is mediated by oxytocin-dependent synaptic plasticity in the medial amygdala. *Biol Psychiatry.*2014 Sep 1;76(5):377-86.

[178] Hou W, Zhang Q, Yan Z, Chen R, Zeh Iii HJ, Kang R, Lotze MT, Tang D. Strange attractors: DAMPs and autophagy link tumor cell death and immunity. *Cell Death Dis.* 2013 Dec 12;4:e966.

[179] Bi P, Ruan S, Zhang X. Periodic and chaotic oscillations in a tumor and immune system interaction model with three delays. *Chaos.* 2014 Jun;24(2):023101.

[180] Skarda CA, Freeman W. *How brain makes chaos in order to make sense of the world Behav Brain Sci* 1987; 10(2):161.

[181] Bernardes AT, dos Santos RM. Immune network at the edge of chaos. *J Theor Biol.* 1997 May 21;186(2):173-87.

[182] Broderick G, Craddock TJ. Systems biology of complex symptom profiles: capturing interactivity across behavior, brain and immune regulation. *Brain Behav Immun.* 2013 Mar;29:1-8.

[183] Pezard L, Nandrino JL. [Dynamic paradigm in psychopathology: "chaos theory", from physics to psychiatry]. *Encephale.* 2001 May-Jun;27(3):260-8.

[184] Smith K. Against homeopathy--a utilitarian perspective. *Bioethics.* 2012 Oct;26(8):398-409.

[185] Levy D, Gadd B, Kerridge I, Komesaroff PA. A Gentle Ethical Defence of Homeopathy. *J Bioeth Inq.* 2014 Jul 19.

[186] Sebastian I. Homeopathy and extraordinary claims--a response to Smith's utilitarian argument. *Bioethics.* 2012 Nov;26(9):504-5.

[187] Milgrom L, Chatfield K. Is homeopathy really 'morally and ethically unacceptable'? A critique of pure scientism. *Bioethics.* 2012 Nov;26(9):501-3.

[188] Chirumbolo S. High diluted molecules and gene expression. *Front Pharmacol.* 2014 Aug 14;5:183.

[189] Chirumbolo S. More on the clinical usefulness of Oscillococcinum. *Eur J Intern Med.* 2014 Jun;25(5):e67.

[190] Chirumbolo S. Oscillococcinum®: Misunderstanding or biased interest? *Eur J Intern Med.* 2014 Mar;25(3):e35-6.

[191] Chirumbolo S. Gelsemine and Gelsemium sempervirens L. Extracts in Animal Behavioral Test: Comments and Related Biases. *Front Neurol.* 2011 May 16;2:31.

[192] Chirumbolo S. Bias and adverse effects of homeopathy: is scientific criticism in homeopathy a "mission impossible"? *Int J Clin Pract.* 2013 Sep;67(9):923-6.

[193] Boiron C. Homeopathy, a tremendous opportunity for medicine! *Eur J Intern Med.* 2011 Feb;22(1):117-8; author reply 118-9.

[194] Turone F. Homoeopathy multinational Boiron threatens amateur Italian blogger. *BMJ.* 2011 Aug 12;343:d5197.

[195] Brien S, Lachance L, Prescott P, McDermott C, Lewith G. Homeopathy has clinical benefits in rheumatoid arthritis patients that are attributable to the consultation process but not the homeopathic remedy: a randomized controlled clinical trial. R*heumatology* (Oxford). 2011 Jun;50(6):1070-82.

[196] Bellavite P. On the plausibility of homeopathic 'similitude'. *Bioethics.* 2012 Nov;26(9):506-7.

[197] Teixeira MZ. Evidence of the principle of similitude in modern fatal iatrogenic events. *Homeopathy.* 2006 Oct;95(4):229-36.

[198] Chirumbolo S. Adverse effects and homeopathy: may remedies yet contain noxious or toxic molecules? *Br J Clin Pharmacol.* 2014 Jul;78(1):184-5.

[199] Chirumbolo S. Homeopathy is not pharmacology. *J Intern Med.* 2013 Dec;274(6):612-3.

[200] Davis MP, Bruera E. Trial design for breakthrough pain: is it ethical to have a placebo in a trial? *Clin Ther.* 2014 May;36(5):814-5.

[201] Sanderson C, Hardy J, Spruyt O, Currow DC. Placebo and nocebo effects in randomized controlled trials: the implications for research and practice. *J Pain Symptom Manage.* 2013 Nov;46(5):722-30.

[202] Bystad M, Bystad C, Wynn R. How can placebo effects best be applied in clinical practice? A narrative review. *Psychol Res Behav Manag.* 2015 Jan 29;8:41-5.

[203] Nitzan U, Bloch Y, Fennig S. Using placebo medications in the clinical setting - an intellectual game or a possible reality? *Isr J Psychiatry Relat Sci.* 2014;51(3):182-7.

[204] Asai A, Kadooka Y. Reexamination of the ethics of placebo use in clinical practice. *Bioethics.* 2013 May;27(4):186-93.

In: Placebo Effects
Editor: Kendra Vaughn
ISBN: 978-1-63482-960-1

Chapter 2

THE PLACEBO AND NOCEBO RESPONSES IN PATIENTS WITH EPILEPSY

***Fabio Giovannelli*[1,*]*, Filippo Sean Giorgi*[2] *and Gaetano Zaccara*[1]

[1]Unit of Neurology, Department of Medicine, Florence Health Authority, Firenze, Italy; and Department of Neuroscience, Psychology, Pharmacology and Child Health (NEUROFARBA), University of Florence, Firenze, Italy

[2]Neurology Unit, Department of Clinical and Experimental Medicine and University Hospital, University of Pisa, Pisa, Italy

ABSTRACT

Placebo and nocebo responses in epilepsy have been mainly investigated by meta-analytic approaches aimed to evaluate the extent of such phenomenon in randomized, controlled, clinical trials. These studies reported placebo response rates (defined as proportion of patients with $\geq$ 50% improvement of seizures compared to baseline observations) ranging from 9.9% up to 15.2%. The proportion of patients with adverse events (AEs) and those withdrawing because of intolerable AEs, as index of nocebo response, were 60.3% and 3.9%, respectively. Moreover, a full evaluation of specific AEs reported by patients receiving placebo has been performed. A number of factors related to the features of patients

* Corresponding author: Fabio Giovannelli, Unit of Neurology, San Giovanni di Dio Hospital, Via Di Torregalli n 3, 50143, Firenze, Italy. E-mail: fabio.giovannelli@unifi.it.

(severity of disease), to the study design, or to non-specific factors (such as year of publication and geographic area), as well as to positive or negative expectations of patients, caregivers and experimenters have been showed to influence placebo and nocebo response in epilepsy. A characterization of these factors is crucial for a better interpretation of study results and to improve design of new clinical trials. All recent data will be presented and discussed in detail.

In addition, as neurobiological studies in epilepsy are lacking, putative mechanisms of placebo and nocebo responses in epilepsy will be hypothesized and discussed along with possible consequences in clinical practice.

Keywords: Epilepsy; Placebo; Nocebo; Antiepileptic drugs; Adverse effects; Meta-analysis; Meta-regression

1. Introduction

Epilepsy is a neurological disorder typically characterized by recurring seizures [1]. The World Health Organization (WHO) indicated that approximately 50 million people worldwide suffer from epilepsy, and partial-onset seizures represent the largest number of cases [2, 3]. Add-on therapy with anti-epileptic drugs (AEDs) is usually effective in approximately two-thirds of patients with epilepsy. About 20 new AEDs have recently been designed for the treatment of partial-onset epilepsy. Registrative studies, which have demonstrated their efficacy and adverse effect profiles [4, 5] and have lead them in the market, have been in all cases performed with a double-blind design aimed to compare the active drug with a placebo in the population of patients with drug resistant, focal epilepsies.

Analysis of these studies may be the only way to assess placebo and nocebo effects in patients with this particular disease which is characterized by the appearance of symptoms due to abrupt brain dysfunction of organic nature although psychological factors are known to play a major role.

In this chapter we define *placebo response as a* positive response to an inert substance induced by expectations [6]. On the contrary, when this response is negative, it can be defined as *nocebo response* [7]. In the context of clinical trials, the therapeutic effect of AEDs depends on the pharmacological properties of drugs but is affected also by other factors. They include spontaneous symptom variation or changes in the natural history of the epilepsy, statistical artifacts such as regression to the mean (i.e. an apparent improvement due to spontaneous fluctuation in seizure frequency), subjective reporting bias, and the psychosocial context of the therapeutic act [8-10]. Moreover, similarly to clinical setting, patient's treatment expectations may represent a crucial aspect with both positive and negative consequences on the outcome of therapy [10].

At present, most of available information on placebo and nocebo responses in epilepsy come from randomized clinical trials (RCTs), during which selected population of drug-resistant patients with focal epilepsies are randomized to treatment with placebo or active drugs in a double-blind condition. Namely, the extent of placebo and nocebo responses in RCTs have been estimated by evaluating response rates (defined as proportion of patients with ≥ 50% improvement of seizures compared to baseline observations) and adverse event profile in patients randomized to placebo arms by meta-analytic approaches.

Meta-analysis provide a picture of the studied phenomenon by a statistical synthesis of the available data from a set of comparable studies. Moreover, meta-regression models allow to explore all sources of heterogeneity and potential factors that may affect outcome measures. Such approach revealed that a number of factors related to the characteristic of patients, to the study design, or to non-specific factors (such as year of publication and geographic area), as well as to positive or negative expectations of patients, caregivers and experimenters, may affect placebo and nocebo response in epilepsy. A full characterization of these factors is crucial for a better comprehension of study results and to improve design of new clinical trials.

In the following sections, available data on the placebo and nocebo responses in RCTs in epilepsy will be separately presented and discussed. Overall the precise determinants of placebo and nocebo response in epilepsy trials remain poorly understood [11].

2. Response Rate in the Placebo Arms of RCTs (Placebo Response)

The first meta-analysis reporting data on placebo response in epilepsy has been performed by Rheims et al. [12] on twenty-seven RCTs conducted in adults patients. Authors reported a mean placebo response rate of 9.9 ± 4.6%. A slightly higher mean percentage of placebo responders, i.e. 12.5% (95% CI: 10.03-14.94%), was subsequently found by Guekht et al. [13].

A more extensive meta-analysis has been recently conducted by Zaccara et al., [14]. Seventy-nine RCTs evaluating twenty licensed and investigational AEDs in a total of 6793 adult patients treated with placebo were included in the analysis. Although in the framework of a high heterogeneity, the mean placebo response observed was 15.2% (95% CI, 13.3-17.1%, range 0-39%) [14].

Interestingly, a similar response to placebo has been reported in patients treated with non-invasive brain stimulation techniques [15]. Namely, the analysis of three placebo-controlled trials evaluating the efficacy of low-frequency repetitive transcranial magnetic stimulation (rTMS) in a total of 63 patients with focal epilepsies, showed a responder rate of 15.8% in patients randomized to the treatment with sham rTMS at the earliest follow-up evaluation [15].

With respect to other diseases, such as depression, neuropathic pain and migraine, in which higher placebo responses have been reported in RCTs, epilepsy shows a relatively modest placebo response. This is likely due to differences in the outcome measures used for the assessment and in the experimental design [16]. Moreover, in trials conducted in focal epilepsies, recruited patients have a long history of therapeutic failures which may be associated with a decreased susceptibility to expectancy-related mechanisms [10].

Another interesting point is the difference between placebo response observed in adults and in children. Several studies in diseases other than epilepsy, indicate an increased placebo effect in children and adolescents [17-19] compared to adult patients. Similarly, Rheims et al. [12] found that percentages of placebo responders in adults and children were significantly different also in drug-resistant epileptic patients with focal epilepsies. In contrast, a recent meta-analysis performed to compare placebo response in adults and in a larger number of studies conducted in pediatric populations, reported a slightly higher percentage of responder in the placebo arms for pediatric RCTs, i.e. 19.7% (95% CI, 16.0, 23.4), but failed to confirm a significant difference [20].

2.1. Factor Influencing Placebo Response in RCTs

A number of factors influencing placebo response in epilepsy RCTs have been identified.

Similarly to that observed for other diseases, also meta-analyses conducted in epilepsy showed increasing responder rates over time (i.e. responder rates significantly higher in more recent than in older studies), as revealed by a positive correlation between responder rates in placebo-treated patients and the year of publication [13, 14, 21]. As higher placebo response may critically reduce the effect size of the active drug, more patients should be recruited in an RCT to demonstrate efficacy of a new AED.

Moreover, some characteristics of recruited patients may influence placebo response. For example, the severity of epilepsy, measured as median number of seizures at baseline, has been reported to be inversely correlated with responder rate [14]. Such data confirm previous findings of a meta-analysis of studies conduced in patients recruited in regulatory RCTs of lacosamide [22]. Namely, four clinical features were significantly associated with lower placebo response: a history of seven or more prior lifetime AEDs compared to fewer lifetime AEDs, an high baseline seizure frequency, prior epilepsy surgery and higher age at diagnosis.

Characteristics of RCTs may also affect placebo response. Regulatory studies include patients from different geographical areas and this may influence placebo response. For example, in a recent RCT assessing perampanel efficacy, an unexplained higher placebo response in South vs. North America was observed [23]. However, an analysis limited to patients recruited in regulatory lacosamide RCTs, showed that patients recruited in the United States had a higher, but not statistically significant chance of entering placebo response than patients from South and Central America [22]. Our analysis aimed to identify whether placebo response systematically differs in different geographical areas (North America, Europe and Asia) failed to show significant differences possibly because only few studies were analyzed [14]. To test the hypothesis that geographical factors or center effects may affect placebo response, data from single centers should be made available by industry.

It has been also shown that placebo response rate increases with the duration of period of evaluation [21]. Moreover, the method of assessment also significantly affect placebo responder rate. In RCTs, analysis of responder rate can be performed for the full duration of double-blind phase (titration plus maintenance) or restricted to maintenance phase only. Interestingly, and for unexplained reasons, the placebo response was significantly higher when the analysis was restricted to the maintenance phase versus the entire treatment period [21].

3. Adverse Event Profile in the Placebo Arms of RCTs (Nocebo Response)

In epilepsy RCTs, a substantial proportion of patients receiving placebo may experience adverse events (AEs) which match those related to active drug [8]. In a clinical setting, treatment-emergent AEs may occur early after starting a new treatment with a negative impact on patients quality of life [24].

The nocebo response in RCTs setting has been estimated by the proportion of patients withdrawing because of AEs, the proportion of patients presenting any AE, and the proportion of patients with specific pre-defined AEs [14, 25].

Our meta-analysis showed that about 3.9% of patients randomized to placebo withdrew from the study due to AEs while 60.3% complained at least one AE during the study [14].

A further characterization of the nocebo response in epilepsy RCTs, revealed that subjective AEs such as somnolence, dizziness and fatigue showed a percentage ranging around 8% while objective AEs such as ataxia, diplopia and tremor occur in around 3% of patients randomized to placebo [25].

It is noteworthy that the method used for the assessment represents a crucial factor influencing the frequency of reported AEs [26]. Namely, using checklists and questionnaires often produce an overestimation of AEs frequency compared to unstructured interviews [27, 28]. For example, in a US study of 200 consecutive outpatients with epilepsy who completed an adverse event profile questionnaire, mean number of AEs per patient was 6.5 [24]. Findings from an Italian naturalistic cross sectional study conducted in 809 consecutive adult patients with refractory epilepsy showed that with the use of a toxicity scale three times as many AEs were identified as in the earlier unstructured interview [28]. Thus such factor should be taken into account in data interpretation.

3.1. Factor Influencing Nocebo Response in RCTs

A great interest has been directed to the evaluation of the factors influencing patients' expectations in the nocebo response occurrence. Particularly, the informed consent procedure in which patients are informed about the possible AEs they may experience during the treatment, has been hypothesized to have a significant impact on their expectations [7]. Different information about adverse events yields different clinical responses [7]. In trials of anti-migraine drugs the class of drugs administrated, i.e. anticonvulsants or non steroidal anti inflammatory (NSAID), has been showed to influence the pattern of tolerability [29]. It has been suggested that the investigator may communicate to the patients the most frequently reported AEs of that class of drugs such as dizziness, fatigue and somnolence for AEDs and gastrointestinal and dry mouth for anti inflammatory drugs. Another factor which may strongly influence nocebo response in some patients may be prior experience with other drugs which caused the observed AE. This experience can lead to sensitization processes that increase both placebo and nocebo responses.

An original findings of meta-analyses conducted by our group is that in all measures used to estimate the nocebo response in epilepsy (i.e. the proportion of patients withdrawing because of AEs, the proportion of patients presenting any AE, and the proportion of patients with specific pre-defined AEs) a significant positive correlation exists between observations reported in the placebo arms and that in the active experimental drug arm [14]. To account for such finding we speculated that the course of the clinical trial may have a role in modulating the tendency to observe with more or less probability a particular event in all patients subsequently recruited, also those in the placebo group. As the knowledge of what is happening in the trial in terms of efficacy and, most important, of tolerability, can only be known by the investigator (for example the AEs observed in previously recruited patients), we proposed that the investigator expectancy may play a relevant role. It is well known that investigator expectancy (Rosenthal effect) can substantially affect the outcome of experimental investigations [30]. Moreover, it should be noted that the issue of tolerability comes to the attention of the investigator much earlier than efficacy. Patients more often complain of AEs or withdraw because of AEs during titration, which is only a few days after starting treatment, while efficacy (or inefficacy) in a patient can be argued after several weeks of treatment.

Such hypothesis is in line with previous data from meta-analysis performed to compare rates of adverse effects reported in the placebo arms of tricyclic antidepressant (TCA) trials and placebo arms of selective serotonin reuptake inhibitor (SSRI) trials [31]. Authors postulated that investigators expected substantial differences between adverse effect profiles of these two classes of drugs. This might explain, at least in part, why more adverse effects were reported in TCA-placebo group compared with SSRI-placebo group [31].

As a consequence, more adverse effects were reported in TCA-placebo groups compared with SSRI-placebo groups [26].

4. Putative Mechanisms of Placebo and Nocebo Responses in Epilepsy

Neurobiological data support the view that different brain mechanisms may be involved in placebo and nocebo responses depending on the disease or the experimental condition [32]. Most of the evidence have been obtained in placebo analgesia showing a key role of endogenous opioid as well as non-opioid systems in placebo pain modulation [32]. Moreover, studies conducted in Parkinson's disease suggest that the placebo response may be mediated by dopaminergic reward mechanisms [33, 34]. Although few studies evaluated mechanisms underlying nocebo response, some evidence suggest that cholecystokinin neurotransmitter system may play a role in nocebo hyperalgesia, likely mediated by anxiety [35]. Moreover, Scott et al. [36] found that nocebo effects may be also associated to a decrease in dopamine and opioid activity in the nucleus accumbens.

In contrast, neurobiological studies on the placebo and nocebo responses in epilepsy are not available, therefore we can only speculate on mechanisms underlying this phenomenon. Mechanisms similar to that involved in placebo response in Parkinson's disease may be active in reducing seizure susceptibility also in epileptic patients when a placebo is administrated. Such hypothesis is based on the role of dopaminergic circuits recently discussed in limbic epileptogenesis has been [37], even though an important limitation is related to the duration of the effect. Namely, in Parkinson's disease such mechanisms are active for a short duration and cannot explain a long lasting placebo response expected during a treatment for epileptic patients. Incidentally, placebo responses have been observed in RCTs lasting up to 37 weeks [14] where these did not decrease or even increase over the time, as suggested from results of a meta-analysis in which it has been observed that placebo response during maintenance period is higher than that observed in all duration (titration plus maintenance) double blind studies [21].

Although we cannot exclude that these and other unknown mechanisms are effective in epilepsy, we believe that in the majority of epileptic patients, placebo response observed in RCTs mainly relies on other factors such as regression to the mean and spontaneous fluctuations of seizure frequency and positive expectations of patients which may generate a subjective feeling of improvement, intentional or unintentional false reporting by patients or caregivers eager to please the investigator, particularly in countries with low-health care resources where participation in a trial assures a diagnostic and therapeutic evaluation which may not be possible otherwise, expectations from investigators which may influence patient's reporting of seizures.

It has also been argued that seizure frequency can be underestimated during the treatment. In a study evaluating safety and efficacy of a long-term implanted seizure advisory system designed to predict seizures in adults with drug-resistant focal seizures [38], it has been reported a substantial disparity between seizures identified by the device and seizure diaries. Namely, objectively identified seizures were more frequent than seizures reported by patients. The authors conclude that more seizures occur than those which patients are aware of.

Moreover, as previously discussed also expectations of investigators or caregivers may affect placebo and nocebo responses. Such hypothesis is also supported by data obtained in clinical trials conducted in animals (e.g., dogs) [39, 40]. All these data indicate that expectations of investigators and caregivers, directly or indirectly (trough influences on patients), are responsible, at least in part, of the placebo response.

CONCLUSION

Notwithstanding the limits of meta-analytic approach, available data suggest that in clinical trials, placebo response account for at least 50% of response to active AEDs [9]. In contrast, nocebo response leads to AED withdrawal in about of 4% of patients whereas in remaining 60% the achievement of the optimal dose may be precluded [14].

In our opinion, placebo-induced expectations likely facilitate a subjective feelings of improvement, without objective change in seizure frequency. However, evidence is lacking and it cannot be excluded that in some cases placebo response may even modify seizure frequency. In patients with epilepsy, a subjective feeling of improvement may set in after taking a new drug. This may have positive and negative consequences. While on one hand it may generate a more optimistic approach to the disease, which alleviates the burden of epilepsy, on the other hand, a belief of efficacy of a drug which is not effective, may prolong ineffective treatments which expose patients to higher risks of AEs, have higher costs, and may preclude attempts with other

AEDs which might be more effective. The false belief of efficacy may also expose patients to higher risks of trauma or, possibly, even death due to uncontrolled seizures. Incidentally, in a meta-analysis of all clinical trials, it has been shown that risk of sudden unexpected death in epilepsy is significantly higher among patients randomized to placebo than in those randomized to active treatment [41].

From our studies emerged that findings in placebo-treated patients of epilepsy RCTs mirrors what happens in active-treated patients. Such effects are likely due to expectations of patients partly generated by information received. However, we proposed that also attitudes and expectations of investigators during the trials may play a more relevant role than that previously hypothesized. Therefore, physicians in clinical practice and investigators involved in clinical trials should be aware that their judgments can be altered by expectations and previous experiences and therefore they should make every effort to minimize such bias.

However, a number of unsolved questions concerning the relationship between placebo or nocebo mechanisms and epilepsy exist. Further studies are needed to better clarify such phenomenon both in clinical trials and clinical practice contexts.

References

[1] (1993) Guidelines for epidemiologic studies on epilepsy. Commission on Epidemiology and Prognosis, International League Against Epilepsy. *Epilepsia*, 34, 592-596.

[2] Ngugi, AK; Bottomley, C; Kleinschmidt, I; Sander, JW; Newton, CR. Estimation of the burden of active and life-time epilepsy, a meta-analytic approach. *Epilepsia*, 2010, 51, 883-890.

[3] Blume, WT; Luders, HO; Mizrahi, E; Tassinari, C; van Emde Boas, W; et al. Glossary of descriptive terminology for ictal semiology: report of the ILAE task force on classification and terminology. *Epilepsia*, 2001, 42, 1212-1218.

[4] Begley, CE; Annegers, JF; Lairson, DR; Reynolds, TF; Hauser, WA. Cost of epilepsy in the United States: a model based on incidence and prognosis. *Epilepsia*, 1994, 35, 1230-1243.

[5] Preux, PM; Druet-Cabanac, M. Epidemiology and aetiology of epilepsy in sub-Saharan Africa. *Lancet Neurol*, 2005, 4, 21-31.

[6] Finniss, DG; Kaptchuk, TJ; Miller, F; Benedetti, F. Placebo Effects: Biological, Clinical and Ethical Advances. *Lancet*, 2010, 375, 686–95.

[7] Colloca, L; Miller, FG. The nocebo effect and its relevance for clinical practice. *Psychosom Med*, 2011,73,598-603.

[8] Murray, D; Stoessl, AJ. Mechanisms and therapeutic implications of the placebo effect in neurological and psychiatric conditions. *Pharmacol Ther*, 2013, 140, 306-18.

[9] Enck, P; Klosterhalfen, S; Weimer, K; Horing, B; Zipfel, S. The placebo response in clinical trials: more questions than answers. *Philos Trans R Soc Lond B Biol Sci*, 2011,366,1889-95.

[10] Zaccara, G; Giovannelli, F; Schmidt, D. Placebo and nocebo responses in drug trials of epilepsy. *Epilepsy Behav*. 2015,43C,128-134.

[11] Rheims, S; Ryvlin, P. Patient and physician preferences: impact on treatment effectiveness. *Epileptic Disord*. 2012,14,242-7.

[12] Rheims, S; Cucherat, M; Arzimanoglou, A; Ryvlin, P. Greater response to placebo in children than in adults: a systematic review and meta-analysis in drug-resistant partial epilepsy. *PLoS Med*. 2008, 5, e166.

[13] Guekht, AB; Korczyn, AD; Bondareva, IB; Gusev, EI. Placebo responses in randomized trials of antiepileptic drugs. *Epilepsy Behav*, 2010, 17, 64-9.

[14] Zaccara, G; Giovannelli, F; Cincotta, M; Loiacono, G; Verrotti, A. Adverse events of placebo-treated, drug-resistant, focal epileptic patients in randomized controlled trials: a systematic review. J Neurol, 2014. [Epub ahead of print].

[15] Bae, EH; Theodore, WH; Fregni, F; Cantello, R; Pascual-Leone, A; Rotenberg, A. An estimate of placebo effect of repetitive transcranial magnetic stimulation in epilepsy. *Epilepsy Behav*, 2011, 20, 355-9.

[16] Hróbjartsson, A; Gøtzsche, PC. Placebo interventions for all clinical conditions. *Cochrane Database Syst Rev*, 2010, (1), CD003974.

[17] Lewis, DW; Winner, P; Wasiewski, W. The placebo responder rate in children and adolescents. *Headache*, 2005, 45, 232-9.

[18] Rothner, AD; Wasiewski, W; Winner, P; Lewis, D; Stankowski, J. Zolmitriptan oral tablet in migraine treatment: high placebo responses in adolescents. *Headache*, 2006, 46, 101-9.

[19] Fernandes, R; Ferreira, JJ; Sampaio, C. The placebo response in studies of acute migraine. *J Pediatr*, 2008, 152, 527-33.

[20] Zaccara, G; Giovannelli, F; Franco, V; Cincotta, M; Tramacere, L; Verrotti, A. Adverse events, placebo and nocebo effects in placebo-

treated paediatric patients with refractory focal epilepsies. Analysis of double-blind studies. *Epilepsy Res*. 2014, 108, 1685-93.

[21] Rheims, S; Perucca, E; Cucherat, M; Ryvlin, P. Factors determining response to antiepileptic drugs in randomized controlled trials. A systematic review and meta-analysis. *Epilepsia*. 2011, 52, 219-33.

[22] Schmidt, D; Beyenburg, S; D'Souza, J; Stavem, K. Clinical features associated with placebo response in refractory focal epilepsy. *Epilepsy Behav*, 2013, 27, 393–8.

[23] French, JA; Krauss, GL; Biton, V; Squillacote, D; Yang, H; Laurenza, A; et al. Adjunctive perampanel for refractory partial-onset seizures: randomized phase III study 304. *Neurology*, 2012, 79, 589-96.

[24] Perucca, P; Gilliam, FG. Adverse effects of antiepileptic drugs. *Lancet Neurol*, 2012,11, 792-802.

[25] Giovannelli, F.; Zaccara, G; Cincotta, M; Loiacono, G; Verrotti, A. Characterization of the adverse events profile of placebo-treated patients in randomized controlled trials on drug-resistant focal epilepsies. *J Neurol*. 2014 Oct [Epub ahead of print]

[26] Baker, GA; Camfield, C; Camfield, P; Cramer, JA; Elger, CE; Johnson, AL; et al. Commission on outcome measurement in epilepsy, 1994–1997: final report. Epilepsia, 1998, 39, 213–31.

[27] Carreño, M; Gil-Nagel, A; Sánchez, JC; Elices, E; Serratosa, JM; Salas-Puig, J; et al. Strategies to detect adverse effects of antiepileptic drugs in clinical practice. *Epilepsy Behav*, 2008, 13, 178–83.

[28] Canevini, MP; De, Sarro, G; Galimberti, CA; Gatti, G; Licchetta, L; Malerba, A; et al. Relationship between adverse effects of antiepileptic drugs, number of coprescribed drugs, and drug load in a large cohort of consecutive patients with drug-refractory epilepsy. *Epilepsia*, 2010, 51, 797-804.

[29] Amanzio, M; Corazzini, LL; Vase, L; Benedetti, F. (2009) A systematic review of adverse events in placebo groups of anti-migraine clinical trials. *Pain*, 146, 261-269.

[30] Rosenthal, R. Experimenter effects in behavioral research. New York: Appleton Century Crofts, 1966.

[31] Rief, W; Nestoriuc, Y; von, Lilienfeld-Toal, A; Dogan, I; Schreiber, F; Hofmann, SG; et al. Differences in Adverse Effect Reporting in Placebo Groups in SSRI and Tricyclic Antidepressant Trials. A Systematic Review and Meta-Analysis. *Drug Saf*, 2009, 32, 1041-56.

[32] Benedetti, F; Carlino, E; Pollo, A. How placebos change the patient's brain. *Neuropsychopharmacology*, 2011, 36, 339-54.

[33] de, la, Fuente-Fernández, R; Ruth, TJ; Sossi, V; Schulzer, M; Calne, DB; Stoessl, AJ. Expectation and dopamine release: mechanism of the placebo effect in Parkinson's disease. *Science*, 2001, 293, 1164-6.

[34] Benedetti, F; Colloca, L; Torre, E; Lanotte, M; Melcarne, A; Pesare, M; et al. Placebo-responsive Parkinson patients show decreased activity in single neurons of subthalamic nucleus. *Nat Neurosci*, 2004, 7, 587-8.

[35] Benedetti; F; Lanotte; M; Lopiano; L; Colloca; L. When words are painful – unraveling the mechanisms of the nocebo effect. *Neuroscience*, 2007, 147, 260–71.

[36] Scott, DJ; Stohler, CS; Egnatuk, CM; Wang, H; Koeppe, RA; Zubieta, JK. Placebo and nocebo effects are defined by opposite opioid and dopaminergic responses. *Arch Gen Psychiatry*, 2008, 65, 220-31.

[37] Bozzi, Y; Borrelli, E. The role of dopamine signaling in epileptogenesis. *Front Cell Neurosci*. 2013, 17, 157.

[38] Mark, J; Cook, MJ; O'Brien, TJ; Berkovic, SF; Murphy, M; Morokoff, A; et al. Prediction of seizure likelihood with a long-term, implanted seizure advisory system in patients with drug-resistant epilepsy: a first-in-man study. *Lancet Neurol*, 2013, 12, 563–71.

[39] Muñana, KR; Zhang, D; Patterson, EE. Placebo effect in canine epilepsy trials. *J Vet Intern Med*. 2010, 24, 166-70.

[40] Muñana, KR; Thomas, WB; Inzana, KD; Nettifee-Osborne, JA; McLucas, KJ; Olby, NJ; et al. Evaluation of Levetiracetam as Adjunctive Treatment for Refractory Canine Epilepsy: A Randomized, Placebo-Controlled, Crossover Trial. *J Vet Intern Med*, 2012, 26, 341–348.

[41] Ryvlin, P; Cucherat, M; Rheims, S. Risk of sudden unexpected death in epilepsy in patients given adjunctive antiepileptic treatment for refractory seizures: a metaanalysis of placebo-controlled randomised trials. *Lancet Neurol*, 2011, 10, 961–8.

In: Placebo Effects
Editor: Kendra Vaughn
ISBN: 978-1-63482-960-1

Chapter 3

NOCEBO PHENOMENA: 'NEGATIVE NON-SPECIFIC EFFECTS'

Maddy Greville-Harris* and Paul Dieppe
[1]PhD, Research Fellow, Centre of Applied Health Research, Psychology Department, University of Southampton, Highfield Campus, Southampton, UK
[2]BSc, MD, FRCP, FFPH, Professor of Health and Wellbeing, University of Exeter Medical School, St Luke's Campus, Exeter, UK

ABSTRACT

The placebo response (improvement in disease or illness in response to an intervention with no active ingredient) is a well-recognised phenomenon, particularly in the context of clinical trials. Its opposite (worsening in response to an 'inactive' intervention) is less well documented and understood, in part because of the difficulties encountered in studying it. However, there is now a considerable literature reporting nocebo responses in trials, in response to medication prescriptions, as well as in response to population-based activities such as the introduction of mobile phones. In addition, and given emphasis in this article, a well-intentioned health care consultation can result in negative outcomes.

---

* Correspondence to Maddy Greville-Harris: m.l.greville-harris@soton.ac.uk

Our research has investigated the role of invalidation, and of feeling unsafe or threatened, on the induction of a nocebo response. Our work has led us to believe that it is easier to induce a negative response than a positive one within healthcare consultations, and that nocebo is more powerful than placebo ('bad is more powerful than good').

We conclude with a brief discussion of the ethical and clinical implications of the nocebo response.

Introduction

A placebo is generally thought of as a medical intervention that has no ingredient considered capable of affecting the target condition for which a patient is being treated. Grunbaum [1] differentiated the effects of any health care intervention into specific and non-specific categories – the specific effects being those for which the intervention is being used (the analgesic effects of a pain relieving drug, for example), and the non-specific effects being the outcomes resulting from all other aspects of the intervention that might affect pain or other health-related outcomes. These non-specific, context effects (or 'placebo' effects) arise from a variety of factors, including: the whole socio-cultural context of the use of the drug, the expectations, health beliefs and prior experiences that the patient brings with them, the environment in which the prescriptions is given, the size, shape and colour of the pills used, and the nature of the interactions between patient and provider [2-4]).

Because of the dominance of drugs and drug trials in current allopathic medicine, placebos have become equated with dummy pills, the 'sugar pill' of common parlance, given to patients in trials to act as the 'control' used to compare with the active drug. It has been consistently observed that people in trial control groups, given such dummy pills with no active ingredient, often get better, a phenomenon described as the 'placebo response' [5-7]. But patients in the 'control' group can also get side effects and other adverse outcomes, and this phenomenon is known as the 'nocebo response' [8]. Kirsch has pointed out that placebo and nocebo 'responses' need to be differentiated from the placebo or nocebo 'effects'. Placebo or nocebo 'effects' are the difference between the good or bad outcomes resulting from the dummy intervention, compared with what would have happened if no intervention had been used at all [9], as shown in Figure 1.

Research on placebo effects has indicated that patient expectations are hugely important in determining the positive outcomes to sham interventions, so it has been assumed that the same will be true of nocebo effects, resulting in some authors defining the nocebo effect as adverse outcomes resulting from negative expectations [10]. In this article we argue for a much wider appreciation of the ability of the context and nature of any health intervention to cause harm, as well as benefit, and thus a reconceptualization of what are now called nocebo effects. For the purposes of this article we will call the phenomena, *'negative non-specific effects'*. We argue towards the end of the article that the negative results from the non-specific aspects of interventions are much more important than the positive ones, even though they have a much lower profile amongst both researchers and those who administer health care interventions.

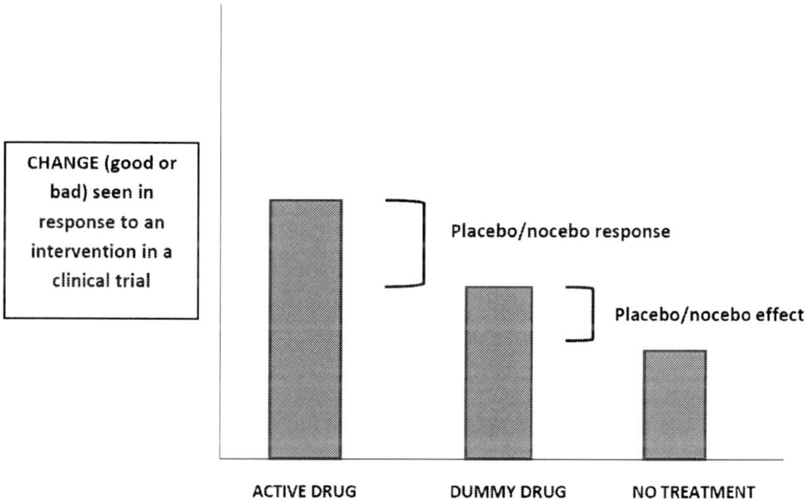

Figure 1. Diagrammatic representation of what is generally meant by the placebo response and the placebo effect when dummy 'control' treatments are compared to an active intervention in a randomised controlled clinical trial (RCT). Exactly the same is true of negative (nocebo) as for positive (placebo) outcomes (after Kirsch [9]).

INVESTIGATING THE NOCEBO EFFECT

It is difficult to investigate the placebo response, because we need to deceive people in order to find out about the effects of a sham or dummy intervention: the subjects of the experiments need to believe that the intervention they are receiving could have some effect. We assume that if people are told that the treatment they are being given has no active ingredient, nothing would happen to them. One 'open placebo' study has been published which suggests that this may not always be the case [11]. In this trial 80 patients with irritable bowel syndrome were randomised to receive no treatment, or to receive open label placebo pills described to the patients as "placebo pills made of an inert substance, like sugar pills, that have been shown to produce significant improvement in symptoms through mind-body, self-healing processes". Those randomised to the placebo pills did better than the control group, suggesting that use of placebos without deception may be effective. However, this needs further exploration, and in general, deception is used in one way or another in most placebo research.

When it comes to nocebo research, we have the added problem of the need to generate adverse effects, something that is generally regarded as highly unethical. It is not surprising, therefore, that the amount of research looking at nocebo effects is even less than that related to placebo effects. Nevertheless, there are a number of instances in which nocebo effects have both been demonstrated and investigated, as outlined in the next section.

Some Contexts and Categories of 'Negative Non-Specific Effects'

The negative effects of interventions that have received clinical and research interest can be differentiated into five main categories:

- The unexpected negative outcomes experienced as a result of any medication
- Negative effects of dummy pills used in trials
- Pain being made more severe in experimental studies
- The negative outcomes that can result from social or population-based interventions
- The negative effects of health care interactions

Negative Responses to Standard Drug Therapy

Although patients taking medication often experience adverse side effects that are not caused by the pharmacological action of the medication itself, this is not often studied and is not well understood [15]. One important contributor to such side effects is the principle of informed consent; healthcare providers must inform patients of possible side effects when they prescribe medications. Yet this disclosure in itself may induce negative non-specific effects [16]. According to Wells and Kaptchuk [16] 'describing one version of what might happen (clinical "facts") may actually create outcomes that are different from what would have happened without this information (another version of "facts")' (p.22). For example, patients told that they would 'feel a bee sting' before having an injection of local anaesthetic, reported more pain than patients who were told the injection would 'numb the area' so that they would be 'comfortable during the procedure' [17]. Many of these adverse effects could be avoided if the patient was not aware that they may occur, or could perhaps be minimised by the manner in which side effect information is provided.

Unexpected negative outcomes that occur as part of routine treatment are thought to be largely due to negative expectations, but classical conditioning can also be the cause. One of us (PD) is a clinical rheumatologist, used to prescribing drugs to patients with inflammatory arthritis- drugs that often cause gastrointestinal side effects. Some patients consistently reported gastrointestinal adverse effects, such as nausea, stomach pains and sickness, even when given tablets designed to have the opposite effects. This, we believe, is due to the fact that so many previously prescribed medications have caused such adverse effects that these patients have become conditioned to respond to any tablet in this way. Similarly, experiments with chemotherapeutic agents have found that people can be conditioned to get nausea and other negative outcomes from the inert drink in which the drug has previously been administered [14]. It is clear, therefore, that negative expectations and/or prior conditioning can lead to adverse effects arising from any pharmacological intervention, and presumably the same is true of other types of medical intervention.

An intriguing experiment was recently reported by Faasse et al, which suggests that adverse effects resulting from the administration of drugs may depend in part on what they call 'social modelling' [18]. 82 University students took part in an experiment in which they were given a dummy beta-blocker tablet supposedly to help them with pre-examination anxiety. The researchers monitored their heart rate and blood pressure responses as well as self-reported anxiety. Participants were randomised to witness a female peer report experiencing side effects or no side effects after taking the same medication. The female students who saw their confederate report side effects experienced many more adverse events than those who saw their peer report no problems. This led the authors to conclude that social modelling of symptoms in response to medications can have a big effect.

The Effects of Dummy Pills Used in Trials

The literature on this aspect of nocebo has been reviewed recently by Data-Franco and Berk [8]. The most striking and consistent literature concerns the side-effects experienced by people given sham drugs in 'blind' trials (trials in which neither the patient not the prescriber knows whether an individual patient is receiving active or placebo medication). The data show a varying prevalence, with a tendency for women to report both a higher frequency and severity of side-effects, and with the adverse events experienced tending to be consistent with those that might be expected from the active ingredient being used in the trial [12]. The explanation that is usually given for these responses is expectation [8].

Again, another important consideration related to negative outcomes in trial control groups is the influence of the consent process. Trial participation is dependent on 'fully-informed' consent, and to be fully informed you must be aware of what might go wrong (as well as right). It is believed that the majority of unwanted adverse symptoms that patients report in clinical trials are often not due to the medication, because comparable effects are seen in the control group [13] but result from the patient being informed of possible side effects. This alters expectations, so informed consent is a powerful intervention in its own right, and one that might contribute hugely to both placebo and nocebo responses in clinical trials as well as in the health care setting.

Pain Made Worse in Experimental Studies

Experimentally induced pain has been a model widely used to explore both placebo and nocebo responses. The advantages of the model include the fact that transient pain can be induced easily in normal subjects, as well as those with diseases, and that provided that fully informed consent is given, such experiments are considered ethical, as there is little likelihood of long term negative outcomes. Many elegant experiments have been carried out using this model, particularly by Benedetti and colleagues in Italy [19-21]. They have shown that it is possible to make pain worse by inducing negative expectations, as well as to produce a positive pain-reducing placebo response in such models [22]. In addition to negative expectations, the presence of anxiety has been shown to be a factor responsible for nocebo responses to pain [23].

Population-Based Interventions Resulting in Negative Outcomes

Nocebo responses are not limited to specific medical interventions or to consultations with healthcare professionals. An early example of the recognition of this phenomenon came from work on 'mobile phone headache' [24, 25]. Many people claim to suffer from headaches as a result of their use of mobile phones. However, numerous studies have shown that the incidence and type of headache induced by mobile phone use is not related to the phone being turned on or off, or the presence of absence of the fields thought to be responsible [26, 27]. Another striking example, investigated by Keith Petrie's group in New Zealand, is the adverse health effects that some people have experienced as the result of the building of wind turbines in their neighbourhoods [28]. It has been suggested that wind turbines cause 'infrasound' which poses health risks [29], and people have complained of a variety of non-specific symptoms, such as nausea, sleep disturbance and headache, which they have attributed to nearby wind turbines [30]. But Crichton et al [28] have put together a compelling, experimentally and epidemiologically based argument, that the symptoms are related to negative stories and expectations about wind turbines and the noise they cause, rather than to the turbines themselves.

The Negative Effects of Health Care Interactions

Most of us have to seek advice and help from medical professionals from time-to-time in our lives. Such events almost always start with a consultation – a one-on-one interaction between the person seeking help and the healthcare provider. Such interactions take place in a wide variety of settings and environments, which can affect the nature of the consultation. And it is our common experience that such interactions can seem positive or negative; sometimes we feel relaxed and safe with the person we are consulting, and feel that we can trust them, but on other occasions we may not experience such positive emotions. Similarly, what is said by the person we are consulting can appear helpful or unhelpful, both at the time, and on later reflection. Within medical education much emphasis is given to communication skills, and to the ways in which healthcare professionals can try to make sure that the consultation is a positive experience, as it is recognised that this can influence patient-related outcomes: we know that healthcare professionals can induce a placebo response through their behaviour. Much less attention has been given to the ways in which healthcare professionals can cause damage, and negative patient-related outcomes – a nocebo response to consultations. We believe, on the basis of our research outlined below, that this is a critical factor in health care and one that deserves a lot more research and attention.

In much of the nocebo literature, authors have concentrated on expectations and/or classical conditioning as the likely explanation for nocebo effects [23, 31, 32]. Yet the potential damage caused by other factors, such as communication, has been largely overlooked. Hauser et al. argue that 'doctor-patient communication....can have considerable consequences, both positive and negative, on the outcome of a course of medical therapy' [33], and we believe that the doctor-patient interaction can be an important facilitator of the nocebo effect. Indeed, there is evidence that patient-doctor communication can be problematic; patients with medically unexplained symptoms for example, report feeling disbelieved and dismissed by their healthcare providers during consultations [34]. Such negative communication can be unintentional; attempts to reassure patients that there is nothing physically wrong with them, can leave the patient feeling dismissed and delegitimized. For patients in considerable pain, such reassurance can communicate to the patient that their experience of pain has not been taken seriously [35]. Our research has been looking at the negative implications of such communication, focusing in particular on the importance of communicating understanding ('validation'), rather than a lack of understanding ('invalidation')- albeit unintentionally- to the patient.

Validating and Invalidating Communication

Validation is a communication strategy developed by Linehan [36] which communicates acceptance and understanding of another's thoughts, feelings, desires or behaviours [37]. In contrast, invalidation is the opposite, communicating a lack of acceptance and understanding to the recipient. Fruzzetti [38] has developed a comprehensive framework of validating and invalidating behaviours in dyadic interactions. Validating behaviours include acknowledging or seeking to clarify what the person has said, or normalising their behaviours. In contrast, invalidating behaviours include not attending to, or dismissing the recipient, insisting on what the other person does or should think or feel, or pathologizing the other's behaviour. Validation is not just empathy (to sense the person's 'world as if it were your own' (p.32) [39] because it focuses not only on understanding another person, but on *communicating* to the other person that you understand and accept them.

Building on previous work [40], we were interested in examining the potential nocebo effects of non-understanding (invalidating) communication. In our experimental research [41] we randomly assigned 90 participants to receive validating, invalidating or no feedback during a series of maths stressor tasks. During the experiment we measured participants' physiological arousal levels, self-reported ratings of mood, perceived safety and willingness to take part in the study again. We found that participants who received invalidating feedback displayed higher levels of physiological arousal, were less willing to take part in the study again and rated their perceived safety levels and mood as significantly lower. There were no significant differences on any of these measures for those who received validating feedback compared with those who received no feedback. This suggests the potentially detrimental and powerful effects of negative (invalidating) communication.

Invalidation as a Nocebo in the Healthcare Setting

Research in the health care setting also supports this idea. We observed and recorded medical consultations in a specialist pain management clinic, and carried out semi-structured interviews with five patients (females with chronic widespread pain) and four healthcare providers (two male and two female). During the patient interviews, we played back excerpts from the consultation and discussed these with the patients, as well as talking about their experiences in medical consultations more generally. Interviews were then analysed using thematic analysis. We found that both patients and providers discussed instances of feeling invalidated by the other party. The patients, for example, described experiences of providers who did not show insight into their condition or invest in them, as well as those who disbelieved or dismissed them. Providers too, described encountering patients who did not believe their diagnosis, who were critical or conflictive, or held entrenched views about their condition and treatment. For both parties, these kinds of interactions had adverse effects. The patients described feeling an increased need to justify their condition, feeling angry or hopeless, and avoiding particular doctors or treatment altogether. Similarly the providers described feeling hopeless in these consultations, dismissing the patient, or referring them on.

It appears that sometimes communication can go wrong during consultations, leaving both parties feeling misunderstood. Although this research is based on a small sample of patients and providers, it is in line with previous research [34, 42-47] and suggests that invalidating consultations may have powerful detrimental effects.

The Role of Social Safety in the Nocebo/Placebo Effect

As well as the emotional and behavioural responses to invalidation (such as feeling hopeless and angry, or avoiding treatment), we have also found that receiving invalidating feedback can affect our physiological responses. We believe that one important mediator of these physiological responses is how *safe* we feel in our social environment. According to Porges' polyvagal theory [48-53] when we perceive the environment as safe we engage the myelinated pathways of the vagal nerve. The myelinated vagal pathway slows our heart rate, reduces blood pressure and decreases levels of autonomic arousal, resulting in a calm visceral state which promotes growth and restoration. Moreover, due to the vagal connection between the heart and the striated muscles of the face and head, this pathway allows the individual to engage in social behaviours. In contrast, when we perceive danger in the environment, visceral states that promote mobilization behaviours occur; we engage our sympathetic nervous system resulting in increased heart rate, and the down-regulation of the striated muscles of the face and head, thus hampering our ability to engage with the social world.

This evolutionary-based theory describes the important physiological responses that occur when perceiving social threat in the environment. According to Porges and others [48, 50, 51, 54, 55], such responses can be detrimental for healing and impede our ability to interact optimally with others. There is some evidence that feeling misunderstood during a social interaction can make us feel less safe. In our experimental research we found that participants who received invalidating feedback described feeling less safe than those who received validating (or no) feedback. This suggests that invalidation (feeling dismissed, misunderstood, delegitimised) decreases feelings of social safety within the environment, which we believe in turn, may mediate these nocebo effects. If feeling less safe leads to sympathetic arousal, which can impede healing [56], one reason that negative social interactions may cause damage, is through the physiological responses that they facilitate.

The Power of Bad Communication is Stronger than Good

In carrying out our research, we fully expected to find that validating communication was helpful and invalidating communication was detrimental. Interestingly, in our experimental study, we found no significant differences in mood, physiological arousal, willingness to take part in the study again or perceived safety levels between those who received validating feedback and those who received no feedback at all. Yet invalidating feedback had detrimental effects on these factors compared with validating and no feedback. This suggests that 'bad' communication has more powerful effects than 'good' communication, and supports the work of Baumeister and colleagues [57].

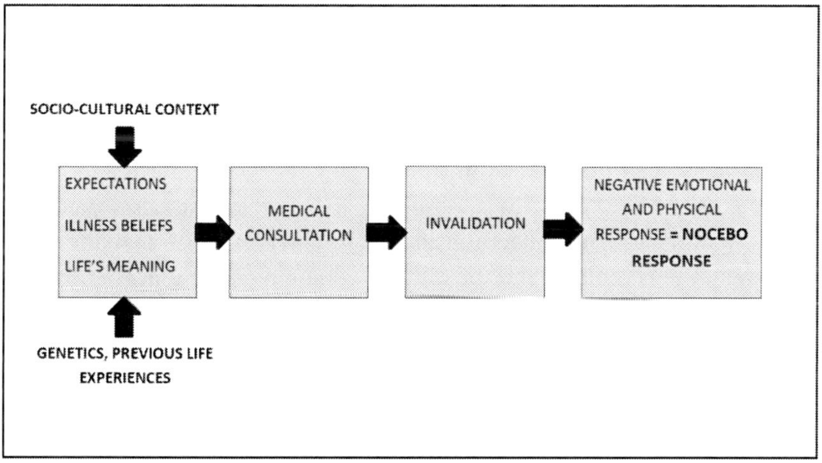

Figure 2. The nocebo response resulting from the medical consultation.

Baumeister et al. [57] suggest that the power of 'bad' is stronger than 'good' in human interactions, and that this serves an evolutionary purpose. In the past (and to some extent today), in order to survive, we needed to be more vigilant to threats within our environment, than to non-threatening stimuli. Thus we have evolved to pay more attention to aspects of our environment that are threatening (even social threats, such as feeling delegitimized or dismissed by another) than to those that are not.

This suggests that perhaps what is important in health communication, is focusing on *avoiding* negative feedback, such as invalidation, rather than focusing on offering positive feedback (for example through empathy, compassion, validation or reassurance). In doing so we may be able to tackle the potential nocebo effects of negative health communication.

Clinical and Ethical Implications

Four key principles of medical ethics have been delineated [58]. They are:

- Non-maleficence - "first, do no harm" (*primum non nocere*).
- Beneficence - a practitioner should act in the best interest of the patient. (*Salus aegroti suprema lex.*)
- Respect for autonomy - the patient has the right to refuse or choose their treatment. (*Voluntas aegroti suprema lex.*)
- Justice - concerns the distribution of scarce health resources, and the decision of who gets what treatment (fairness and equality).

Some authors suggest that non-maleficence should have first place in the hierarchy of these principles.But modern health care often does harm [59]. In this article we suggest that in addition to the inadvertent harm caused by mistakes and misuse of modern health care interventions, that the act of prescribing an intervention, and the clinical communication that is at the heart of all health care can also cause harm, and that 'harm is more powerful than good' [60].

Our review of the nocebo literature, as well as our experimental work, suggest that there may be two key issues that clinicians need to be aware of if they are to avoid inadvertent doing harm to their patients when consulting:

- Both the patient and the doctor need to feel 'safe' during any healthcare interaction, and as far as is possible anxiety should be alleviated
- Any words or behaviours that might be interpreted as invalidating by the patient must be avoided.

Feeling Safe

Most people feel anxious when consulting with a healthcare professional. There is an intrinsic power differential (the professional holds more power than the patient), and there is the fear that the professional might find something wrong with us, or suggest a treatment that will frighten and threaten us. Sadly, it is often the case that the health care professional is also feeling anxious or unsafe during a consultation, as he or she may be scared of making a mistake, of missing an important diagnosis, or of not fulfilling the needs of the health care funders, as well as those of the patient.

So, in general, health care consultations do not feel 'safe'. But the work of Porges and colleagues [49-51] indicates that when we feel threatened we cannot communicate well. Perhaps this is why so many patients say that 'the doctor did not understand me', or 'I was not listened to properly', or 'I did not understand what they said'. And the nocebo literature indicates that anxiety can make a negative response to the non-specific effects surrounding any consultation or prescription more likely, by increasing pain perception for example [23].

So, we believe that an essential thing for practitioners to strive for is a feeling of safety and avoidance of anxiety and threat, both within themselves as well as in their patients. Paying attention to the whole environment, finding out how to make any individual feel relatively at ease with you, and shutting out any fears of your own, should be attended to. Unfortunately much of what the medical profession does has the absolute opposite effect – our consulting rooms and treatment centres are full of frightening looking instruments for example, and doctors and health care professionals can easily bring a sense of foreboding.

Antenatal care is a case in point. It ought be a joyous business in which the mother to be is made to feel safe and cared for, but Michelle Odent, one of the proponents of water birthing [61], has said that much of what we do in our clinics is 'antenatal scare' rather than antenatal care (personal communication). He points out that instead of concentrating on the positives, we often talk about what might go wrong and what needs to be done to avoid disasters, thus leading to negative expectations amongst pregnant women, perhaps leading to more antenatal problems than would occur if we did nothing.

Doctors are told that they must inform patients of the likely risks of any medicine or surgery that they are suggesting. But how we do that and what we say puts the patient at risk of suffering from the risk that has been explained, because of a nocebo effect. That presents us with a clinical and ethical dilemma, made more difficult by the ease of access that patients have to information on the web and elsewhere about all the things that can go wrong with their treatments. The clinical author of this article (PD), prior to giving up his practice, tried to avoid undue emphasis on side effects when prescribing medicines to his patients, and attempted to enhance the likely placebo response to them, rather than inducing a nocebo response, but he often felt that he was walking on a tightrope between the ethical principles of doing no harm, and of respect for autonomy.

Avoiding Invalidation

The other conclusion from our work is that clinicians must try to avoid invalidating their patients. Much attention is paid to compassion and empathy in medicine, but you can be compassionate and empathic without your patient realising it. If understanding and acceptance is not *perceived* by the patient, inadvertent invalidation can ensue, leading to potential negative outcomes for the patient. We know that in all aspects of our lives, simple phrases that we use all the time in an attempt to be kind and supportive can misfire. For example, one person will often say to another who is in distress, 'I know how you must feel', which can be infuriating for the person on the receiving end, who might feel hurt, and like saying - 'how could x possibly know how I feel, they are not going through what I am'. The consequences of such mistakes in a clinical setting can clearly be particularly damaging, leading to worsening of disease or illness. How can healthcare professionals avoid invalidating their patients? We were struck by the wisdom of one of the clinicians whom we interviewed for the research outlined above, who said that he 'simply wanted to understand the patient with him as best he could'. It may be that simple, just being present with someone else and genuinely wanting to understand their plight and their point of view. Maybe that could help us all comply with the ethical principle of 'primum non nocere'.

Acknowledgments

We would like to thank the National Institute of Health Research (NIHR) in the UK, the Peninsula School of Medicine and Dentistry, Exeter University

Medical School, and The Institute for Integrative Health (www.tiih.org USA) for financial and Institutional support.

We are also grateful to our research collaborators, including Professor Tom Lynch, Dr Roelie Hempel and Dr Anke Karl for their contributions to the original research summarised here.

REFERENCES

[1] Grunbaum, A., The Placebo Concept in Medicine and Psychiatry. *Psychological Medicine,* 1986. 16(1): p. 19-38.

[2] Kaptchuk, T.J., et al., Components of placebo effect: randomised controlled trial in patients with irritable bowel syndrome. *British Medical Journal*, 2008. 336(7651): p. 999-1003.

[3] Howick, J.,Placebo misery. Escaping from placebo prison. *British Medical Journal*, 2009.338.

[4] Doherty, M. and P. Dieppe, The "placebo" response in osteoarthritis and its implications for clinical practice. *Osteoarthritis & Cartilage*, 2009. 17(10): p. 1255-1262.

[5] Wampold, B.E., et al., The placebo is powerful: estimating placebo effects in medicine and psychotherapy from randomized clinical trials. *Journal of Clinical Psychology*, 2005. 61(7): p. 835-854.

[6] Kirsch, I. and G. Sapirstein, Listening to Prozac but hearing placebo: A meta-analysis of antidepressant medication. *Prevention & Treatment*, 1998. 1(2): p. 2a.

[7] Finniss, D.G., et al., Biological, clinical, and ethical advances of placebo effects. *The Lancet*, 2010. 375(9715): p. 686-695.

[8] Data-Franco, J. and M. Berk, The nocebo effect: A clinicians guide. *Australian & New Zealand Journal of Psychiatry*, 2013. 47(7): p. 617-623.

[9] Kirsch, I., The placebo effect revisited: Lessons learned to date. *Complementary Therapies in Medicine*, 2013. 21(2): p. 102-104.

[10] Colloca, L. and F.G. Miller, The Nocebo Effect and Its Relevance for Clinical Practice. *Psychosomatic Medicine*, 2011. 73(7): p. 598-603.

[11] Kaptchuk, T.J., et al., Placebos without deception: a randomized controlled trial in irritable bowel syndrome. *PloS One*, 2010. 5(12): p. e15591.

[12] de la Cruz, M., et al., Placebo and nocebo effects in randomized double-blind clinical trials of agents for the therapy for fatigue in patients with advanced cancer. *Cancer,* 2010. 116(3): p. 766-774.

[13] Bingel, U. and T. For the Placebo Competence, Avoiding nocebo effects to optimize treatment outcome. *JAMA*, 2014. 312(7): p. 693-694.

[14] Bovbjerg, D.H., et al., An experimental analysis of classically conditioned nausea during cancer chemotherapy. *Psychosomatic Medicine,* 1992. 54(6): p. 623-637.

[15] Barsky, A.J., et al., Nonspecific medication side effects and the nocebo phenomenon. *JAMA*, 2002. 287(5): p. 622-627.

[16] Wells, R.E. and T.J. Kaptchuk, To tell the truth, the whole truth, may do patients harm: the problem of the nocebo effect for informed consent. *The American Journal of Bioethics*, 2012. 12(3): p. 22-29.

[17] Varelmann, D., et al., Nocebo-induced hyperalgesia during local anesthetic injection. Anesthesia & Analgesia, 2010. 110(3): p. 868-870.

[18] Faasse, K. and K.J. Petrie, The nocebo effect: patient expectations and medication side effects. *Postgraduate Medical Journal*, 2013: p. postgradmedj-2012-131730.

[19] Amanzio, M. and F. Benedetti, Neuropharmacological dissection of placebo analgesia: expectation-activated opioid systems versus conditioning-activated specific subsystems. *The Journal of Neuroscience,* 1999. 19(1): p. 484-494.

[20] Amanzio, M., et al., Response variability to analgesics: a role for non-specific activation of endogenous opioids. *Pain,* 2001. 90(3): p. 205-215.

[21] Benedetti, F., The opposite effects of the opiate antagonist naloxone and the cholecystokinin antagonist proglumide on placebo analgesia. *Pain,* 1996. 64(3): p. 535-543.

[22] Enck, P., F. Benedetti, and M. Schedlowski, New insights into the placebo and nocebo responses. *Neuron*, 2008. 59(2): p. 195-206.

[23] Colloca, L. and F. Benedetti, Nocebo hyperalgesia: how anxiety is turned into pain. *Current Opinion in Anesthesiology*, 2007. 20(5): p. 435-439.

[24] Oftedal, G., et al., Mobile phone headache: a double blind, sham-controlled provocation study. *Cephalalgia,* 2007. 27(5): p. 447-455.

[25] Hocking, B., Preliminary report: symptoms associated with mobile phone use. *Occupational Medicine*, 1998. 48(6): p. 357-360.

[26] Koivisto, M., et al., GSM phone signal does not produce subjective symptoms. *Bioelectromagnetics,* 2001. 22(3): p. 212-215.

[27] Rubin, G.J., et al., Are some people sensitive to mobile phone signals? Within participants double blind randomised provocation study. *British Medical Journal,* 2006. 332(7546): p. 886-891.

[28] Crichton, F., et al., Can expectations produce symptoms from infrasound associated with wind turbines? *Health Psychology*, 2014. 33(4): p. 360.

[29] Knopper, L.D. and C.A. Ollson, *Health effects and wind turbines: A review of the literature*. 2011: BioMed Central.

[30] Pierpont, N., Wind turbine syndrome: A report on a natural experiment. 2009: K-Selected Books Santa Fe, NM, USA.

[31] Jensen, K.B., et al., Nonconscious activation of placebo and nocebo pain responses. *Proceedings of the National Academy of Sciences*, 2012. 109(39): p. 15959-15964.

[32] Pollo, A., et al., Preventing motor training through nocebo suggestions. *European Journal of Applied Physiology*, 2012. 112(11): p. 3893-3903.

[33] Häuser, W., E. Hansen, and P. Enck, Nocebo phenomena in medicine: their relevance in everyday clinical practice. *Deutsches Ärzteblatt International,* 2012. 109(26): p. 459.

[34] Werner, A. and K. Malterud, It is hard work behaving as a credible patient: encounters between women with chronic pain and their doctors. *Social Science & Medicine*, 2003. 57(8): p. 1409-1419.

[35] Linton, S.J., L.M. McCracken, and J.W.S. Vlaeyen, Reassurance: Help or hinder in the treatment of pain. *Pain*, 2008. 134(1-2): p. 5-8.

[36] Linehan, M.M., Validation and psychotherapy. In Bohart, A C. & Greenberg, L S. (Eds), Empathy reconsidered: New directions in psychotherapy, pp. 353-392,1997.

[37] Fruzzetti, A.E. and J.M. Worrall, Accurate expression and validating responses: A transactional model for understanding individual and relationship distress. *Support Processes in Intimate Relationships*, 2010: p. 121-150.

[38] Fruzzetti, A.E., *Validating and Invalidating Behaviour Coding Manual*. 2010: University of Nevada.

[39] Rogers, C.R., The Necessary and Sufficient Conditions of Therapeutic Personality-Change, (Reprinted from Journal of Consulting Psychology, Vol 21, Pg 95-103, 1957). *Journal of Consulting & Clinical Psychology,* 1992. 60(6): p. 827-832.

[40] Shenk, C.E. and A.E. Fruzzetti, The Impact of Validating and Invalidating Responses on Emotional Reactivity. *Journal of Social and Clinical Psychology*, 2011. 30(2): p. 163-183.

[41] Greville-Harris, Does Feeling Understood Matter? The Effects of Validating and Invalidating Interactions. 2013: Peninsula College of Medicine and Dentistry. p. Doctoral Thesis.

[42] Eccleston, C., A.C.D. Williams, and W.S. Rogers, Patients' and professionals' understandings of the causes of chronic pain: Blame, responsibility and identity protection. *Social Science & Medicine*, 1997. 45(5): p. 699-709.

[43] Corbett, M., N.E. Foster, and B.N. Ong, Living with low back pain - Stories of hope and despair. *Social Science & Medicine*, 2007. 65(8): p. 1584-1594.

[44] Reid, S., et al., Medically unexplained symptoms - GPs' attitudes towards their cause and management. *Family Practice*, 2001. 18(5): p. 519-523.

[45] Frantsve, L.M.E. and R.D. Kerns, Patient-provider interactions in the management of chronic pain: Current findings within the context of shared medical decision making. *Pain Medicine,* 2007. 8(1): p. 25-35.

[46] Fitzpatrick, R., Telling patients there is nothing wrong - Unless their true fears are addressed, diagnostic tests may leave them more anxious than before. *British Medical Journal*, 1996. 313(7053): p. 311-312.

[47] Wileman, L., C. May, and C.A. Chew-Graham, Medically unexplained symptoms and the problem of power in the primary care consultation: a qualitative study. *Family Practice*, 2002. 19(2): p. 178-182.

[48] Porges, S.W., Orienting in a Defensive World - Mammalian Modifications of Our Evolutionary Heritage - a Polyvagal Theory. *Psychophysiology*, 1995. 32(4): p. 301-318.

[49] Porges, S.W., The Polyvagal Theory: The phylogenetic substrates of a social nervous system. *International Journal of Psychophysiology*, 2000. 35(1): p. 2-2.

[50] Porges, S.W., The polyvagal theory: phylogenetic substrates of a social nervous system. *International Journal of Psychophysiology*, 2001. 42(2): p. 123-146.

[51] Porges, S.W., The Polyvagal Theory: phylogenetic contributions to social behavior. *Physiology & Behavior*, 2003. 79(3): p. 503-513.

[52] Porges, S.W., The polyvagal perspective. *Biological Psychology*, 2007. 74(2): p. 116-143.

[53] Porges, S.W. and G.F. Lewis, The polyvagal hypothesis: common mechanisms mediating autonomic regulation, vocalizations and listening. *Handbook of Mammalian Vocalization: An Integrative Neuroscience Approach*, 2010. 19: p. 255-264.

[54] Cohen, S., Social relationships and health. *American Psychologist*, 2004. 59(8): p. 676.

[55] Beckes, L. and J.A. Coan, Social baseline theory: The role of social proximity in emotion and economy of action. *Social & Personality Psychology Compass,* 2011. 5(12): p. 976-988.

[56] Kemeny, M.E., The psychobiology of stress. *Current Directions in Psychological Science*, 2003. 12(4): p. 124-129.

[57] Baumeister, R.F., et al., Bad is stronger than good. *Review of General Psychology,* 2001. 5(4): p. 323.

[58] Gillon, R., Medical ethics: four principles plus attention to scope.British Medical Journal, 1994. 309(6948): p. 184.

[59] Illich, I. and D. McCarthy, *Limits to medicine: medical nemesis: the expropriation of health*. 1976: Marion Boyars London.

[60] Greville-Harris, M. and P. Dieppe, Bad is more powerful than good: the nocebo response in medical consultations. *The American Journal of Medicine*, 2014.

[61] Odent, M., Birth under water. *The Lancet*, 1983. 322(8365): p. 1476-1477.

INDEX

#

21st century, 40

A

access, 74
accounting, 12
acquired immunity, 15, 18
ACTH, 15, 16, 36, 37
active compound, 5
AD, 57
adaptation, 41
adhesion, 16
adipose, 19
adipose tissue, 19
adolescents, 50, 57
adrenocorticotropic hormone, 15
adults, 49, 50, 55, 57
adverse effects, vii, 1, 8, 24, 25, 31, 44, 53, 58, 64, 65, 69
adverse event, viii, 47, 49, 52, 53, 58, 65, 66
aetiology, 56
age, 11, 18, 51
alkaloids, 5
allergy, 16
alternative medicine, vii, 1, 2, 3, 24
alters, 40, 66
alveolar macrophage, 35
ambassadors, 4
amygdala, 19, 35, 36, 41, 43
analgesic, 62
anatomy, 16
anger, 14
antagonism, 36
antidepressant, 75
antidepressant medication, 75
antiepileptic drugs, 57, 58
anxiety, 13, 14, 16, 17, 19, 23, 32, 33, 34, 35, 36, 37, 38, 39, 40, 54, 65, 67, 72, 73, 76
anxiety disorder, 33, 35
ARC, 41
arousal, 11, 13, 15, 35, 69, 70
Asia, 51
assessment, 29, 50, 51, 52
ataxia, 52
ATP, 20, 41
attachment, 21
attitudes, 11, 20, 56, 78
autoimmunity, 42
autonomy, 72, 74
avoidance, 73
awareness, 2, 7, 8, 10, 13, 18, 20, 23, 24

B

back pain, 78
bacteria, 20
barriers, 32

base, 29
basic research, 32
behaviors, 35
benefits, 42, 44
bias, 9, 11, 22, 24, 49, 56
bioethics, 23
blogger, 44
blood, 36, 65, 70
blood pressure, 65, 70
blood vessels, 36
bowel, 31
brain, 14, 16, 17, 19, 20, 21, 27, 34, 38, 39, 40, 41, 43, 48, 50, 54, 58
breast cancer, 36
bronchitis, 32

C

CAM, v, vii, 1, 2, 3, 6, 7, 9, 10, 22, 24, 27, 32
cancer, vii, viii, 2, 16, 31, 76
carbohydrate, 41
cardiovascular disease, 16
cardiovascular function, 15, 19, 21
cardiovascular system, 40
caregiver, vii, 1
caregivers, viii, 48, 49, 55
cell death, 43
cell differentiation, 15
cell line, 36
central nervous system, 18
chaos, 43
chemical(s), 2, 3, 4, 6, 7, 9, 10, 24, 27
chemotherapeutic agent, 65
chemotherapy, 76
children, 31, 50, 57
chronic fatigue, 33
chronic fatigue syndrome, 33
cities, 30
civil rights, 26
civilization, 26
classes, 53
classical conditioning, 65, 68
classification, 56
clinical trials, viii, 4, 9, 11, 22, 47, 48, 49, 55, 56, 57, 58, 61, 66, 75, 76
CNS, 16, 34, 42
cocaine, 38, 40
cognition, 14, 33
cognitive process, 20
cognitive processing, 20
common sense, 6
communication, 10, 32, 33, 34, 39, 68, 69, 70, 71, 72
communication skills, 68
community, 5
compassion, 33, 72, 74
complementary medicine, viii, 1
complexity, 12, 23
compounds, 5, 25
comprehension, 49
conditioning, 65, 76
conference, 4
confounders, 9, 12
connectivity, 21, 43
consciousness, 8
consensus, 23, 27
consent, 66
consolidation, 8
constituents, 39
consulting, 2, 13, 14, 18, 21, 67, 72, 73
control group, 33, 62, 64, 66
controlled studies, 31
controlled trials, 9, 28, 31, 32, 45, 50, 57, 58
conviction, 2, 9, 20, 23
coping strategies, 18, 39
corticotropin, 36
cortisol, 15, 16, 19, 36
cough, 32
criticism, 5, 23, 27, 44
cross sectional study, 52
cultural beliefs, 11, 26
cure, viii, 1
CV, 34
cytokines, 28

D

damages, 4

danger, 70
database, 24, 25
defence, 17, 18, 19, 30
deficit, 20
dendritic cell, 36
depression, 14, 19, 32, 33, 34, 50
despair, 78
dialysis, 40
diet, 40
diplopia, 52
disclosure, 65
diseases, 5, 50, 51, 66
disorder, 14, 48
dissociation, 36
distress, 14, 74, 77
distribution, 25, 72
dizziness, 52, 53
doctors, 4, 70, 73, 77
dogs, 55
dominance, 62
dopamine, 54, 59
dopaminergic, 54, 59
down-regulation, 13, 19, 70
drug addict, 17
drug addiction, 17
drug withdrawal, 17
drug-resistant epilepsy, 59
drugs, 4, 11, 48, 49, 53, 58, 62, 65, 66

E

EBM, vii, viii, 2, 11
education, 6, 23, 68
emotion, 14, 33, 39, 79
emotional reactions, 14
emotional responses, 18, 33
emotional state, 14
empathy, 10, 43, 69, 72, 74
endocrine, 10, 13, 14, 16, 18, 24, 42
endothelial cells, 16
energy, 39, 41
enuresis, 31
environment(s), 8, 10, 12, 14, 17, 21, 27, 31, 62, 67, 70, 71, 73
environmental stimuli, 31
epidemiologic, 56
epidemiologic studies, 56
epilepsy, vii, viii, 47, 48, 49, 50, 51, 52, 53, 54, 55, 56, 57, 58, 59
epileptogenesis, 54, 59
epithelial cells, 21, 42
equality, 72
equilibrium, 27
ethanol, 37, 38
ethics, 45, 72, 79
etiology, 34
Europe, 4, 51
evidence, vii, viii, 2, 3, 5, 7, 9, 12, 15, 16, 22, 24, 25, 29, 43, 54, 55, 68, 70
evidence based medicine, vii, viii, 2
evil, 25
experimental condition, 54
experimental design, 50
expertise, 5, 8, 27
exposure, 36

F

facial expression, 41
facilitators, 32
fairness, 72
false belief, 56
fasting, 40
fat, 41
fear(s), 12, 14, 41, 73, 78
feelings, 55, 68, 70
financial, 26, 75
flight, 19
fluctuations, 54
fluoxetine, 32
focal seizure, 55
food, 36
food intake, 36
force, 29, 56
Ford, 31
forecasting, 18, 38
foundations, 25
freedom, 26
functional MRI, 14
funds, 3

G

GABA, 19
gene expression, 44
general practitioner, vii, 1, 5, 32
genes, 39
genome, 18
genus, 31
geometry, 41
glia, 17, 38
glucocorticoids, 15, 34
glutamate, 19
God, 30
gray matter, 16
growth, 36, 42, 70

H

headache, 67, 76
healing, viii, 1, 2, 4, 7, 13, 17, 22, 31, 42, 64, 70
health, viii, 2, 7, 13, 20, 23, 24, 25, 27, 30, 40, 55, 61, 62, 63, 64, 66, 67, 68, 69, 72, 73, 79
health care, viii, 23, 26, 55, 61, 62, 63, 64, 66, 68, 69, 72, 73
health care professionals, 73
health effects, 67
health problems, 24
health risks, 67
healthcare consultations, ix, 62
heart rate, 65, 70
hepatic failure, 31
herbal medicine, 23, 27
heterogeneity, 49, 50
hippocampus, 15, 16, 35
history, 30, 48, 50, 51
homeopathy, viii, 1, 2, 3, 4, 6, 7, 8, 9, 10, 14, 22, 24, 27, 28, 29, 30, 31, 32, 33, 44
homeostasis, 3, 8, 15, 16, 17, 21, 39
homeostatic response, vii, 1
honesty, 5
hormone(s), 14, 16, 19, 20, 22, 28, 41
host, 20
human, 8, 14, 16, 22, 36, 38, 39, 42, 71
human health, 22
human interactions, 71
hypertrophy, 40
hypoglycemia, 42
hypothalamus, 16, 40
hypothesis, 16, 17, 25, 28, 51, 53, 54, 55, 78

I

iatrogenic, 4, 44
ideal, 25
identity, 78
immigrants, 27
immune activation, 16
immune defense, 17
immune function, 12, 13, 15, 18, 34, 35
immune regulation, 21, 43
immune response, 10, 13, 14, 16, 17, 18, 20, 38
immune system, 14, 33, 34, 36, 43
immunity, 14, 16, 18, 20, 35, 37, 39, 43
imprinting, 19
in vitro, 9
incidence, 56, 67
individual differences, 38
individual personality, 18
individuals, 9, 11, 24
inducer, 11, 23
induction, ix, 62
industry, 51
inflammation, 16, 18, 34, 39
inflammatory arthritis, 65
inflammatory disease, 36
informed consent, 11, 52, 65, 66, 76
ingredients, 25
inhibition, 16, 36
instinct, 14
insulin, 40, 42
integration, 39
internalization, 35
intervention, viii, 17, 33, 61, 62, 63, 65, 66, 72
intracellular calcium, 40

irritable bowel syndrome, 10, 14, 28, 29, 33, 64, 75
isolation, 30
issues, viii, 2, 14, 24, 26, 72
Italy, 1, 47, 66

L

lactose, 5, 8
landscape, 4, 26
landscapes, 7
laws, 6, 25, 29
lead, 8, 9, 18, 27, 48, 53, 65
learning, 43
leptin, 19, 40, 41
lifetime, 51
ligand, 15
light, vii, viii, 2, 15, 17, 28
light cycle, 15
limbic system, 33
local anesthetic, 76
localization, 42
locus, 16
Luo, 43
lymphocytes, 35

M

machinery, 18
majority, 26, 54, 66
man, 25, 42, 59
management, 10, 78
mass, 5, 26
mass media, 26
mast cells, 14, 34
materials, 4
matter, 4, 8, 9
measurement, 58
mechanical stress, 4, 23
median, 51
mediation, 36
medical, vii, 1, 2, 3, 4, 7, 9, 10, 12, 14, 22, 26, 28, 33, 62, 65, 67, 68, 69, 71, 72, 73, 78, 79
medical science, 26
medication, viii, 61, 64, 65, 66, 76
medicine, vii, viii, 1, 4, 6, 7, 8, 10, 22, 24, 27, 30, 32, 44, 62, 73, 74, 75, 77, 79
Mediterranean, 30
medulla, 20
memory, 13, 21, 22, 43
mental processes, 20
meta-analysis, 23, 28, 31, 49, 50, 51, 52, 53, 54, 56, 57, 58, 75
metabolic syndrome, 40
metabolism, 18, 39
metals, 5
metaphor, 29
mice, 19, 34, 35, 39, 40, 41
microbiota, 14, 38, 39
migration, 16, 36
milk sugar, 5
mind-body, 30, 64
mission, 36, 44
misunderstanding, 6, 26
misuse, 72
mitogen, 16
mobile phone, viii, 61, 67, 76, 77
modelling, 65
models, 15, 20, 28, 67
modern society, 26
mole, 6, 30
molecules, 3, 11, 13, 21, 44
mood disorder, 14, 15, 17, 19
morphine, 37
MR, 33
muscles, 70

N

nanoparticles, 31
National Academy of Sciences, 77
natural killer cell, 15
nausea, 65, 67, 76
negative consequences, 49, 55
negative effects, 64
negative mood, 39
negative outcomes, vii, viii, 1, 61, 64, 65, 66, 74

negative response, ix, 62, 73
neocortex, 20
nephropathy, 40
nerve, 70
nervous system, 78
neural network(s), 14
neural system, 14
neurobiology, 14, 33
neuroinflammation, 37
neurons, 20, 35, 38, 59
neuropathic pain, 50
neuropeptides, 3, 12, 14, 16, 17, 18, 19, 22, 28, 35
neuro-pharmacology, vii, viii, 2
neurophysiology, 12, 19, 20, 27
neuroscience, 28
neurotransmitter, 54
new media, 36
New Zealand, 67, 75
nitric oxide, 42
nocebo, vii, viii, ix, 1, 14, 17, 23, 24, 45, 47, 48, 49, 52, 53, 54, 55, 56, 57, 59, 61, 62, 63, 64, 66, 68, 69, 70, 71, 72, 73, 74, 75, 76, 77, 79
norepinephrine, 20
North America, 51
NPS, 15, 34, 35
nuclei, 16, 20
nucleus, 54, 59

O

obesity, 15
opioids, 76
opportunities, 34
optimism, 18, 39
optimists, 18
organism, 3
osteoarthritis, 75
outpatients, 52

P

paediatric patients, 58
pain, 12, 15, 35, 39, 43, 45, 54, 62, 65, 66, 68, 69, 73, 76, 77, 78
pain management, 69
pain perception, 73
palliative, vii, viii, 2, 5, 22, 27, 32
palliative care, vii, viii, 2, 5, 22, 27, 32
parallel, 10
participants, 69, 70, 77
pathology, 18, 25
pathophysiology, 19
pathways, 70
peptide, 15, 21, 35, 37, 38
peripheral nervous system, 15
personal communication, 73
personality, 39
phagocytosis, 16, 35
pharmaceutical, vii, 1, 6, 24
pharmacological treatment, 2
pharmacology, vii, viii, 1, 2, 4, 6, 11, 30, 44
phenotype(s), 15, 35
physicians, 4, 7, 56
physics, 43
physiological arousal, 69, 71
physiological mechanisms, 12
physiology, 16
pilot study, 28, 37
placebo, vii, viii, ix, 1, 2, 3, 4, 6, 7, 8, 9, 10, 12, 13, 14, 15, 16, 17, 19, 20, 21, 22, 23, 24, 27, 28, 29, 30, 31, 32, 33, 39, 45, 47, 48, 49, 50, 51, 52, 53, 54, 55, 56, 57, 58, 59, 61, 62, 63, 64, 66, 68, 74, 75, 76, 77
Placebo effect, vii, 1, 59
placebo response, vii, viii, 2, 6, 8, 9, 10, 11, 12, 13, 14, 17, 21, 22, 24, 27, 47, 48, 49, 50, 51, 54, 55, 57, 58, 61, 62, 63, 67, 68, 74
plants, 25
plasticity, 35
plausibility, 3, 44
PM, 56
polarization, 36
polymorphism, 19, 21, 27, 40
polymorphisms, 42
polypeptide, 38
population, viii, 19, 48, 49, 61, 64

positive attitudes, 9
positive correlation, 51, 53
positive emotions, 67
positive feedback, 72
post-traumatic stress disorder, 36
prejudice, 2, 23, 24, 25
preparation, 6
principles, 72, 74, 79
probability, 53
professionals, 67, 74, 78
prognosis, 56
pro-inflammatory, 15
prolactin, 19
proliferation, 35, 36
protection, 78
protein kinases, 16
Prozac, 75
psychiatry, 31, 43
psychobiology, 79
psychology, vii, viii, 2
psychopathology, 43
psychosomatic, 3, 7, 10
psychotherapy, 75, 77

Q

quality of life, 52
query, 25
questionnaire, 11, 32, 52

R

Ramadan, 40
RE, 38
reactions, 27
reactive oxygen, 16
reactivity, 22
reading, 2
reality, 45
reasoning, 14
reception, 7
receptors, 17, 19, 21, 27, 36, 38, 39, 40
recognition, 43, 67
recovery, vii, 1, 3, 7, 13, 14, 17, 26, 27
regression, 48, 49, 54
regression model, 49
relaxation, 42
relevance, 57, 77
relief, 7
repair, 20
reputation, 28
researchers, 3, 7, 12, 27, 63, 65
resilience, 17, 18, 21, 36, 38
resolution, 7, 11, 13
resources, 55, 72
response, vii, viii, ix, 1, 2, 6, 8, 9, 10, 11, 12, 13, 14, 15, 17, 20, 21, 22, 24, 27, 34, 38, 41, 42, 44, 47, 48, 49, 50, 51, 52, 53, 54, 55, 57, 58, 61, 62, 63, 66, 67, 68, 71, 73, 74, 75, 79
restoration, 70
RH, 36
rheumatoid arthritis, 44
rheumatologist, 65
rights, 26
risk(s), 42, 55, 56, 73
rules, 6

S

safety, 55, 69, 70, 71, 73
salts, 5
schizophrenia, 42
school, 6
science, 26
scope, 79
SCT, 32
secretion, 15
sedative, 11, 13, 17
seizure, 49, 51, 54, 55, 59
seizures, viii, 47, 48, 49, 51, 55, 56, 58, 59
selective serotonin reuptake inhibitor, 53
semi-structured interviews, 69
sensitization, 38, 40, 53
septic shock, 42
septum, 16, 36
services, 32
severity of disease, viii, 48
sex, 11, 18

sham, vii, 1, 2, 4, 5, 6, 7, 9, 10, 27, 50, 62, 63, 66, 76
shape, 62
showing, 18, 54
shyness, 23
side effect(s), viii, 1, 5, 62, 64, 65, 66, 74, 76
signaling pathway, 41
signals, 7, 17, 77
sleep disturbance, 67
SNP, 15
social behavior, 41, 78
social behaviour, 21, 70
social cognition, 20, 41
social environment, 70
social interactions, 3, 21, 71
social psychology, vii, 1
solution, 27
somnolence, 52, 53
SP, 33
species, 3, 16
state(s), 4, 6, 17, 40, 70
statistics, 11
stimulation, 20, 50, 57
stimulus, 17
stoichiometry, 6
stomach, 65
stratification, 11
stress, 5, 12, 13, 14, 16, 17, 18, 19, 21, 27, 34, 35, 36, 37, 38, 39, 40, 42, 79
stress coping ability, 39
stress response, 14, 16, 17, 21, 28, 37
stressors, 18, 39
style, 21, 38
sub-Saharan Africa, 56
substrate(s), 16, 78
suppression, 41
susceptibility, 50, 54
sympathetic nervous system, 70
symptoms, 7, 14, 34, 48, 64, 66, 67, 68, 76, 77, 78
synaptic plasticity, 43
syndrome, 31, 37, 77
synthesis, 49

T

T regulatory cells, 20
target, 5, 11, 15, 27, 62
techniques, 50
testing, 11
therapeutic effects, 25
therapeutic targets, 42
therapeutics, 5, 23, 24, 30
therapy, vii, 1, 2, 3, 4, 7, 8, 9, 10, 12, 18, 20, 22, 24, 27, 28, 37, 48, 49, 68, 76
thoughts, 68
threats, 71
thymus, 42
toxicity, 23, 52
toxicology, 5
trafficking, 14, 15, 34
training, 77
trait anxiety, 33
trauma, 56
traumatic brain injury, 34
treatment, 9, 11, 14, 20, 27, 29, 31, 32, 33, 48, 49, 50, 51, 52, 53, 54, 55, 56, 57, 59, 63, 65, 69, 70, 72, 73, 76, 77
tremor, 52
trial, 10, 11, 28, 29, 30, 31, 32, 33, 44, 45, 53, 55, 62, 63, 64, 66, 75
tricyclic antidepressant, 53
tumor, 43

U

UK, 61, 74
United States, 51, 56
unstructured interviews, 52
upper respiratory tract, 32
USA, 38, 75, 77

V

validation, 68, 72
vasopressin, 20, 41, 42
vector, 8
vitamins, 11

vocalizations, 78
vulnerability, 38

W

walking, 74
water, 3, 24, 25, 73, 79
weakness, 8, 26
weapons, 5, 25
web, 74
well-being, 42
wind turbines, 67, 77
withdrawal, 17, 38, 55
World Health Organization (WHO), 48
worldwide, 48
wound healing, 20, 41